Jonas Greene

The crown won but not worn

Jonas Greene

The crown won but not worn

ISBN/EAN: 9783337273255

Printed in Europe, USA, Canada, Australia, Japan

Cover: Foto ©Suzi / pixelio.de

More available books at **www.hansebooks.com**

THE

CROWN WON BUT NOT WORN;

OR,

M. LOUISE GREENE,

A STUDENT OF FIVE YEARS

AT KENT'S HILL, ME.

BY

JONAS GREENE.

BOSTON.
1868.

It being the object of the writer to circulate this pamphlet as extensively as possible, he offers it at a very low price, and has made arrangements for the sale and delivery of the same at the following places, viz.:

S. H. COLESWORTHY,
Bookseller, Stationer, and Dealer in Paper-Hangings, Engravings, Picture Frames, and Fancy Articles,
92 EXCHANGE ST., PORTLAND, MAINE.

T. M. VARNEY,
Bookseller and Stationer, and Dealer in Paper-Hangings and Fancy Goods,
No. 6 LISBON ST., LEWISTON, MAINE.

Orders can be directed to either of the above houses. Price 50 cents per copy. A fair discount will be made to those who buy to sell again.

For further information, please inquire at the above houses, or of JONAS GREENE, PERU, MAINE.

PREFACE.

WITH an aching heart, pierced by the keenest arrows of affliction — with fondly cherished hopes blighted — with feelings of sensibility stung to the very quick by the wrongs and injustice which I feel have been done to a near and dear one, as also to myself and my family, I come before you, kind readers, to tell the sad story of my bereavement and my afflictions. I cannot promise you a literary work. If I can present my story of sorrow, my ideas, and views in language that you can comprehend, you will please overlook my awkward style, and want of literature; and you will "pardon something" to the feelings of a bereaved parent. If I shall appear too zealous in the performance of what I feel to be a duty, I will say to you in the language of Job, — "Hear now my reasoning, and hearken to the pleadings of my lips. Suffer me that I may speak; and after that I have spoken, mock on."

The reading portion of the community, generally, in Maine, and thousands out of this State, have heard of the sad tragedy which transpired at Auburn, near Lewiston, not long since: how M. Louise Greene, a student at the Female College at Kent's Hill, Me., left that institution in a wretched state of mind, on the 23d day of May, 1866, travelled to Lewiston, was seen weeping in Auburn, purchased poison, and mysteriously disappeared; how her father, for many weary and anxious days and weeks, searched in and around Lewiston for his lost child; how he employed detectives, circulated handbills and photographs all over the State; while the kind and sympathizing people of Lewiston, Auburn, Lisbon, and other places generously assisted him in many ways, and by hundreds, in searching the wood, the canals, and river to no purpose; and how her bleached remains were accidentally discovered in a lonely spot in the forest, in Auburn, in October following. They have also seen, in some of the journals of the day, paragraphs, afloat in the country, containing the statement that she was detected in pilfering on Kent's Hill, and committed suicide. This is nearly all that the public generally know of the matter, except what busy tongues, and sometimes prejudiced, have breathed, often incorrectly, into the public ear. Thus, thousands, who otherwise would never have heard her name, heard it, for the first time, coupled with infamy and disgrace.

PREFACE.

This M. Louise Greene was our daughter, our oldest child, — who for twenty-two years had been the recipient of a father's indulgent care, a mother's kindest affections, — one whom we loved and doted on, and for whose physical comfort and intellectual culture and improvement we had been sparing of neither pains nor money. Her kind affections ever clung to us, as the tendrils of the vine cling to the oak which protects it. While living, she looked to us for counsel and protection; and though now dead and lost to us forever, as a father I will be faithful to her memory, and protect it, as far as in me lies, against false stigma and unjust reproach. I have carefully and candidly investigated this affair with the zeal and scrutiny of a deeply interested father, and have formed the opinion that my daughter was the victim of *prejudice, improper treatment, erroneous or injudicious management, or culpable neglect.* This is the settled conviction of my mind, whether real or imaginary, from which I cannot recede after months of reflection. To me it appears that some party or parties other than herself are culpable and responsible before God, if not before human laws, for this sad and afflicting occurrence.

"To err is human." If I am in error, after giving the facts and circumstances on which I base my opinion, — if the public shall decide that I have no cause, — I stand corrected. In view of the condition of the case, and of the many rumors and statements that had been sent afloat, seemingly for effect, to exonerate the culpable and reflect on the character of my child, — after gathering up her bleached yet precious remains from the forest, where they had lain in silence for months, and given them a proper burial, — I felt that I still owed an important duty to her memory, which I could not go down to the grave and leave unperformed. This duty was to lay before the public, in an intelligible form, a portion of the circumstances and facts which led me to form the opinion I have before expressed, that others may, in a measure, have the means of judging for themselves whether or not I have reasons for my conclusions, and whether or not my daughter was guilty of such enormous offences that her earthly hopes and future prospects should have been blighted and forever extinguished.

THE CROWN WON BUT NOT WORN.

The charges, or allegations, preferred against Louise, as far as I have been advised, were, in substance, these: that in her and her chum's room were found several articles of wearing apparel that were not her own, but belonged to others connected with the institution;—that she took five dollars in money from the room of one of the students;—that she had in her possession a skeleton key.

I propose now to introduce to my readers some facts, circumstances, testimony, letters, and certificates, and leave them, after a careful and candid perusal, to form their own opinions, and judge for themselves whether or not the following propositions are not amply sustained, namely: That the printed rules of the institution at Kent's Hill, "*to have all articles of clothing put in the wash plainly marked with the owner's name,*" was not enforced or adhered to, but that many articles sent to the wash by teachers, students, and even the help, were unmarked;—that much of the clothing could be recognized only by the quality of the cloth, or the peculiar make, stitches, or hems;—that articles not unfrequently got exchanged, and frequently lost, and that exchanges would naturally and innocently occur; — that for students to take articles from the unmarked pile, not their own, when their own were missing, was not only practised, but allowed, if not advised, by those having charge of that department;—that the articles found in L.'s and her mate's room, of which she had any knowledge, and which were not hers, were there by necessity, and not by theft, her own being gone;—that Miss Case and others claimed and took from L.'s and her chum's room some unmarked articles, claiming them as their own, when the chances are equal that they were Louise's;—that there is no proof that all the articles found in that room, and said to belong to others, were there by any act of L.'s, or that they were all there at the time she left, and that all those articles not her own, of which she had any knowledge, she took without any concealment, in lieu of her own, with no intention of keeping them; — that, at the time of taking the five dollars, she was suffering under partial, if not serious mental aberration, and the act was to her a mystery, no less than to her fellow-students, who knew her character, and to her friends everywhere; and that while she could not account for the act, she did not equivocate nor deny it, but confessed and restored without hesitation, when no evidence or proof was attempted to be brought against her; — that up to this occurrence, from her childhood, she had sustained, both at home and abroad, an irreproachable character; — that she was a professor of Christianity, and lived a virtuous life; — that in searching and examining to fix the guilt of theft upon her, but little leniency or feeling of mercy was manifested towards her; — that attempts were made, while in her " distracted state of mind," to fix upon her the theft of other things which had been missed, and to impress upon her already bewildered mind the " enormity of the crime" of which they accused her; — that she was accused, tried, condemned, and virtually expelled from the school, — as she understood it, — only two weeks before she expected to graduate, without the benefit of counsel or assistance, or a consultation with father, mother, or friends, and informed by Dr. Torsey, that "she had better leave that day," the very day on which she did leave; — that she left that day in the morning, in a state of extreme mental excitement, in her soiled every-day apparel, after divesting herself of her jewelry, and taking nothing but her reticule with her; — that it was known to Dr. T. that she had so left in the forenoon, and concern and fears were expressed to him that she would destroy herself before night; yet no means were taken to watch, follow, or protect her, until her sister, at six o'clock in the afternoon, was sent home, a distance of twenty-five miles in a direction opposite to that L. had taken, to give me information, where she did not arrive till twelve o'clock that night; — that the skeleton key was given her years before, by a student, and kept as a kind of keepsake; and that while having the key was charged against her as a crime, no attempt has ever been made to prove that " she ever used it wrongfully;" — that a prejudice had existed against her, which had been indulged previous to this last affair; — that threats had been made to her, seemingly on account of this prejudice; — that she had suffered under such threats, till there existed in her mind a presentiment that she should never graduate, which had been frequently expressed to her friends; — that in fact she did not find at that institution that " safe and pleasant home" which she had been promised by their circulars; but that, being driven to despair by cruel or indiscreet acts, she was left, by her promised protectors, with indifference, to self-destruction.

In order that my readers may understand the position, condition, and standing of Louise at the time this affair occurred, which commenced on the 21st and terminated on the 23d day of May, 1866, I will give a brief outline of the history of her connection with this institution.

In March, 1861, we carried our daughter, M. Louise, to Kent's Hill, Readfield, Maine, where she entered, as a student, the Maine W. Seminary, located at that place. After a preparatory course of two years, she entered the Female College department, for a three years' course of hard study. She accomplished all the studies, and advanced in all the branches she was required to study, to the satisfaction of her teachers and friends. She successfully studied Latin, French, German, and various other studies required in the course, together with book-keeping, drawing, wax-work, pencil-drawing, and oil painting.

A large number of drawings and oil paintings, executed by her, are left in our hands, which will attest to her proficiency in these branches, and to her genial powers to accomplish much in the fine arts.

When she was three years of age she was sick for a long time, and it was with the utmost care and exertion that we succeeded in saving her life. Again, from the age of twelve to seventeen, her health was extremely poor; so feeble that she lost much of the advantage and opportunity of common-school education.

At an early age she exhibited much tact and aptness in learning, especially in spelling. At the age of twelve, she composed and wrote, unaided by any one, quite an interesting story, which was published at the time. She soon became much interested in literature, and desired a liberal education. We wished the same (when I say *we*, the kind reader will understand that I mean myself, and the afflicted and loving mother of our deceased child), but did not think her health would admit of the attempt until she was seventeen years of age, when we took her, hesitatingly, to that *religious* institution, being somewhat influenced and induced to this step by the promise and inducement held out in their circular, which gave us the assurance of our there finding " a safe and pleasant home " for our daughter.

For the purpose of showing the blandishment of that assurance, and the fidelity with which, in my case, it has been carried out, I will quote a few sentences from the circular, which is now before me : —

" Most of the teachers board with the students, and no reasonable pains are spared to promote the comfort and improvement of the boarders. Parents may feel assured that their sons and daughters will find here a safe and pleasant home. Students will furnish their own sheets, pillow-cases, towels, and toilet soap; and they should see that every article for washing is plainly marked with the owner's name."

Louise continued a student at this institution until May 23, 1866. She had been successful in her studies, the goal of her ambition was almost reached, and she expected to graduate with honor in two weeks, and receive her diploma. I had no notice of her being in any trouble at school until the evening of May 23, at twelve o'clock. At midnight my third daughter, Chestina, arrived home in a state of extreme excitement, and informed me of the case, and that L. had left the Hill, in an awful state of mind, and gone towards Lewiston. I was informed that she was accused of taking things not belonging to her.

Subsequently I had a specification of these charges from the pen of Dr. T. himself. In a letter to me dated June 30, 1866, he says: "The facts, I believe, are these: Louise sent, at different times, bundles of clothing to the wash, from which were taken by the wash-girl five articles of clothing not hers. In her room were found nine or ten articles, some of them marked, and some of them not having been sent to the wash,—some of them belonging out of the building. Before they were shown her, she denied she had such articles in her room. The money she took and put out of her hands at once. For three years she had kept a skeleton key opening all of the students' rooms."

Prof. Robinson, in a letter dated November 12, 1866, makes the following statement: "The facts in the case are these: after as private an investigation as possible, Miss Greene acknowledged that she had taken several articles that did not belong to her; also, that she had taken money from one of the young ladies; also, that she had had in her possession, for two years, a false key, which would open most all the students' rooms in the college."

The public now have before them all the charges made against my daughter by the authorities of the institution at Kent's Hill, in the language of the president, and one other member of the faculty.

It will be noticed that the first was written to me, at a time when it seemed possible that my daughter was yet alive, while the latter was written to another person, after it was known that L.'s tongue was forever silent. It is a bold and positive statement, not qualified by an "I believe," of which, in its proper place, I will take further notice before I have done.

These charges have been reiterated and circulated, and, in their circulation, have been magnified and put in their worst possible form, until a portion of the community have been led to the conclusion that her character was truly so infamous, that her friends' mouths were so completely closed, that they dare not appear before the public in her defence. Certain talkative persons have said: "Mr. Greene dare not make a statement of her case to the public." Even certain Methodist clergymen, as I am informed, have alluded to this matter in their churches, reiterating Dr T.'s fourteen or fifteen counts against L., evidently with prejudice against the deceased, or to clear Dr. T. and the faculty from censure.

The misconstruction put upon the language of L.'s letter to her class, — brief extracts only being given to the public, — the misquotation of her letter, and other damaging insinuations and acts, have determined me to lay that letter, and some others, before the public, that public opinion may have some more reliable base than incorrect rumors, or pretended and prejudiced quotations.

It is not that I seek controversy, or would willingly enter the arena before the public uncalled by duty; but that I seek at the tribunal of public opinion that justice to my loved, lost, and unfortunate child which was denied her elsewhere; and I feel confident that, before this Superior Bench, though the heavens fall, it will be awarded her, however high in community may stand those who would deny her it.

You will bear with me patiently, kind readers, when you consider that almost all the direct and important testimony in this sad case is in the possession of those whose fame and interest might require that its dark features should be withheld from public gaze; and that she who was the recipient of the wrong — if wrong was done her — now sleeps in death. Her silent tongue can make no reply, nor testify as to what grating or burning words crushed her hopes, broke her heart, distracted her brain, and severed her ties to life forever.

You will be aware that I shall be under the necessity of going over much ground to get at the circumstances and facts bearing on this case, in order to give the public a proper understanding of the whole affair.

As to the character of Louise, I cannot, perhaps, better express my views, knowledge, and opinion, than to repeat what we said to Dr. T. at a faculty meeting, at which myself and wife were present, one week after L. left the Hill. In answer to the charges there brought against her we said: "We do *know* that a more honest, upright, and truthful girl than was L., when she came here, never came under your care. She was strictly honest from a child; and if she is now dishonest you have made her so. She has been under your care and control three-fourths of the time for five years past, and you are, in a great measure, responsible for her character."

Dr. T., in the course of the conversation that day, told us that hitherto our daughter's character had been irreproachable. Miss Case, the preceptress, told me, in substance, the same, on the second day after L. left. She said, in substance, that no suspicion had ever rested on L., and that she would as soon have thought of any one of the teachers being suspected as she. Mr. and Mrs. Daggett, each, distinctly, made similar statements as to her good character and standing up to Monday night, May 21st, two days only before she left. I have noticed that, while none of those who first accused L. of misdeeds, and examined into the matter, have ever denied the truth of the statement made to me respecting her former good character, the "facts" of her misdeeds are brought prominently before the public on every opportune occasion; and this other important fact, to the benefit of which she was and her memory is entitled, is not even alluded to

To show the truthfulness of the statements just alluded to, respecting her good character, I will lay before the reader a few certificates from those with whom she boarded while teaching five terms of school, one yearly, at each vacation while attending college. It will be readily seen that few, except her parents, could have a better opportunity than they of ascertaining her true character.

CERTIFICATE OF CITIZENS OF ROXBURY.

"The undersigned, inhabitants of School District No. 2, in the town of Roxbury, do hereby certify that Miss M. Louise Greene, of Peru, taught our school in the summer of 1860. She boarded with us during the whole term of her school. We can truthfully, and do most cheerfully, say that Miss Greene was strictly honest and truthful in all things during her stay with us. She was a social, agreeable, and affectionate member of our family while stopping with us, and gave good satisfaction as a teacher.

"Her moral character stood high and above reproach in this community. Many of us in this school district have known her from her childhood, and we never heard a word against her character until certain reports reached us since she left Kent's Hill in May last.

"AMASA RICHARDS, School Agent.
JANE RICHARDS.

"*Roxbury, Dec.* 1866."

"We can truly indorse all Mr. Richards and his wife have said, in relation to Miss Greene, and to the best of our knowledge we believe her to have been honest and truthful in all things.

"JOHN HUSTON,   STILLMAN A. REED,
ARTHUSA HUSTON,   JOHN RICHARDS,
JOHN REED,   LOUISE RICHARDS,
HANNAH D. REED,   VIRGIL P. RICHARDS."

CERTIFICATES OF CITIZENS OF MEXICO.

"We, the undersigned, inhabitants of School District No. 3, in the town of Mexico, do hereby certify that M. Louise Greene, of Peru, taught our school in the summers of 1863 and 1865. We, Benjamin Allen and wife, certify that she boarded with us the whole of the term of her school, in 1863, and that we do cheerfully and heartily say that Miss Greene sustained an unblemished character. She was strictly honest and truthful in all things during the time she stopped in our family. She was an affectionate, social, and agreeable member of our family. She sustained the same agreeable manners in the school, and throughout the district, giving general satisfaction as a teacher.

"BENJAMIN ALLEN, School Agent, 1863.
SALLY ALLEN."

"I roomed and slept with Miss Greene this whole term, and, in my opinion, a better girl than L. scarce ever lived. I greatly loved and respected her. I am the daughter of Mr. B. Allen.

"LOVINA S. RICHARDS."

"We, the subscribers, Victor M. Abbott and wife, do certify that Miss Greene boarded in our family the whole term of her school in 1865. We can truthfully say that a more social, agreeable, and accomplished girl than she then was, is not known to us. We cheerfully and confidently say to the public that we know she was strictly honest and truthful during her stay with us. She was very particular in small, as well as in larger, matters and things, — the most so of any person we ever had in our house. She gave full and perfect satisfaction as a teacher, and was loved and much respected by all the citizens of this neighborhood.

"VICTOR M. ABBOT, School Agent, 1865,
E. A. ABBOT.

"*Mexico, Dec.* 1866."

"Every article of jewelry, belts, buckles, trinkets, and fancy articles of various descriptions, which I owned, were in my bureau-drawers, and other boxes, in the room which Miss Greene occupied, and in which she slept all the time she boarded with us; and all were left unlocked, open, and at her view, at all times. Nothing was missed or disturbed by her during her stay with us.

"E. A. ABBOT."

"We cheerfully indorse all that Messrs. Allen and Abbot and their wives have said, as to the qualifications and accomplishments of Miss Greene, and the general satisfaction she gave, as a teacher, in our district.

"Her moral character stood high, and above reproach, in our district, and in this town. No tongue of slander ever uttered aught against her, for truth and honesty, during her stay with us, in the summers of 1863 and 1865. She was loved and respected by all.

"DURA BRADFORD,   NERI D. B. DURGIN,
LOIS BRADFORD,   HENRY W. PARK,
WM. M. HALL,   BENJAMIN STORER,
C. E. HALL,   ELIZA L. STORER,
MARY A. BROWN,   LUCY RICHARDS."

"In 1863, I visited Miss Greene's School, and gave her the best report of any teacher in town.

"L. S. RICHARDS,
"*Chairman of S. S. Committee of Mexico in 1863.*"

CERTIFICATES OF CITIZENS OF PERU.

"I hereby certify that Miss M. Louise Greene taught the Summer School in district No. 9, in Peru, in 1862. She boarded in my family during the term. I can truly say, she was truthful and strictly honest during her sojourn with us. I never had a more particular, honest, and straight-forward person in my family. I have known Miss Greene for sixteen years, and never heard anything against her character, except what has come from Kent's Hill since May last. I believe her to have been one of the best of girls. She was the pride of her parents, and an honor to the society and community in which she lived.

"EUNICE TRASK.
"*Peru, Dec.* 1866."

"We, the undersigned, inhabitants of the School-District before named, so far as we know, or believe, can fully indorse all Mrs. Trask has said, in regard to the character and good standing of Miss Greene. We had known her for a long time, in the store and post-office kept by her father. As a teacher, scholar, and public reader, she had scarcely an equal in this community.

"B. F. OLDHAM,   DANIEL OLDHAM, JR., (School Agent).
COLUMBUS OLDHAM,   SOPHRONA OLDHAM,

SARAH OLDHAM, DANIEL OLDHAM,
SIDNEY OLDHAM, PRISCILLA OLDHAM,
JOANNA OLDHAM, P. F. OLDHAM,
FREEMAN IRISH, MARY J. OLDHAM,
ALMEDA IRISH, WM. COX,
S. F. IRISH, LOUISE COX,
LORENZO IRISH, THADDEUS OLDHAM,
ROSE IRISH, THADDEUS OLDHAM, JR.,
LYSANDER FOSTER, SARAH P. OLDHAM,
JOHN OLDHAM."

"We, the undersigned, inhabitants of School-District No. 4, in the town of Peru, do hereby certify, that Miss M. Louise Greene taught the school in our district, in 1864. She boarded in our family during the term, and we can truly say that she was strictly honest and truthful in all things, during her sojourn with us. We never had a more social, pleasant, and agreeable boarder in our house.

"Having known Miss Greene for seventeen years past, ever since she was five years of age, we freely testify that we never heard a word against her moral character, until after she left Kent's Hill, May 23, 1866. We were acquainted with her in the store and post-office kept by her father, and knew her as a scholar and teacher, and never knew aught against her.

"GEORGE W. WHITE, (School Agent),
POLLY K. WHITE.

"*Peru, Dec.*, 1866."

"We can cheerfully indorse all that Mr. and Miss White have said, relative to the character and standing of Miss Greene in this town and community.

"Her fine accomplishments and brilliant powers of mind, made her an ornament and honor to the community and society in which she moved."

" E. G. AUSTIN, THOMAS BURGESS,
WM. A. AUSTIN, ELIZABETH BURGESS,
A. L. HAINES, OTIS WYMAN,
LYDIA AUSTIN, MARY A. WYMAN,
JUDITH AUSTIN, S. S. WYMAN,
LORENZO KNIGHT, MEHITABLE A. WYMAN,
RELIEF E. KNIGHT."

I will here state that in the year 1849 I became a resident, and went into trade in the town of Peru, my place being central in the town, and but a few rods from the house where the town meetings are holden. I have kept the central post-office of Peru all of the time since I moved into this town. Having no boys to assist me, and L. being naturally active and expert with the pen, when at home, was much in the store, assisting me in the post-office, and in waiting on customers, frequently having the whole care and charge in my absence,—thereby becoming acquainted with a great portion of the citizens of the town.

To show the tone of public opinion in her own town, where she has been known from her childhood, I will introduce to the public a certificate of prominent citizens of Peru, who, from the circumstances just named, have had good opportunities of knowing the character of Louise, and they well understand the sentiments and feelings of the people generally in this vicinity concerning her. These are citizens who have held places of honor and trust in this town, within a few years past, and many of them are well known to the public.

CERTIFICATE OF PROMINENT CITIZENS OF PERU.

"We, the undersigned, citizens of Peru, hereby certify that Miss M. Louise Greene, the young lady whose tragical death occurred in the woods in Auburn, sometime in the month of May last, under such painful circumstances, had been a resident of Peru from her childhood. From personal acquaintance and public report, we knew her to be a girl of irreproachable and unblemished character, and of unsullied reputation. Her amiable disposition and affability of manners won for her general respect and esteem. She had the reputation of being an excellent and accomplished scholar, and a competent and successful teacher. Her truthfulness, honesty, integrity, virtue, and fidelity were never subjects of doubt or suspicion in this community.

"Being naturally kind-hearted, and of a very sensitive temperament, she was generous and charitable, and a ready sympathizer with suffering humanity.

"While we freely and unhesitatingly bear testimony to the virtue and good character of this lamented young lady, justice to her memory impels us to say, that in our opinion, whatever unfortunate circumstance or occurrence might have operated, directly or indirectly, as the primary cause of her untimely end, it was not her fault or crime, but her misfortune.

"*Town Officer for* 1866.

   Selectmen.

      Andrew J. Churchill (Ex-Mem. of S. S. Committee).
      Isaac Chase (Ex-Member of Legislature).
      Henry S. McIntire (Ex-Mem. of Leg.)

   Town Clerk.

      Sumner R. Newell (Ex-mem. of Leg. and Chairman of S. S. Committee).

   Town Treasurer.

      William H. Walker (Ex-mem. of S. S. Committee).

   S. S. Committee.

      S. G. Wyman.
      Charles B. Woodsum (Cons. and Collector).
      Wm. K. Ripley (Ex-Selectman).

   Clergymen.

      William Woodsum.
      Samuel S. Wyman.
      Peter Hopkins, Jr.

   Ex-Officers of the Town.

      William Woodsum, Jr., Trial Justice (Ex-Clerk).
      L. H. Maxim, M. D. (Ex-S. S. C.)
      L. D. Delano (Ex-S. S. C.)
      Daniel Hall (Cons. and Col. 1867. Ex-S. M.)
      Thomas I. Demerite (Ex-mem. L. Ex-S. M.)
      Wm. B. Walton (Ex-mem. Leg.)
      Otis Wyman (Ex-S. M. and Ex-S. S. C.)
      Benjamin Lovejoy (Ex-S. M.)
      Cyrus Dunn (Ex-S. M.)
      James Barrows (Ex-S. M.)
      Wm. K. Greene (Ex-S. S. C.)
      Samuel Holmes (Ex-mem. L. and Ex-S. M.)
      Benjamin Allen (Ex-S. M.)

IRA WORMELL (Ex-Cons. and Col.)
CHARLES F. DESHON (Ex-S. M.)
WINSLOW WALKER (Ex-S. M. and Ex-Clerk).
JABEZ M. PHILLIPS (P. M. E. Peru).
MERRILL KNIGHT (S. M. 1867, Ex-S. S. Com.)

Public School Teachers.

WM. S. WALKER,   H. ALBERT HALL,
MERCY C. LUNT,   ELISHA S. WYMAN,
WILLIAM P. BRACKETT, JR., SARAH M. BRACKETT,
A. M. KNIGHT (Member of S. S. C. 1867.)
MARTHA A. HOPKINS,   OLEVIA HOPKINS,
MARY A. CARTER,   BENJ. F. WALTON,
ADDIE H. DUNN,   NOAH HALL,
PHEBE F. CHURCHILL."

The reader perhaps may ask, How did it happen that, contrary to the rules of the institution, requiring "every article for the wash to be plainly marked," your daughter's clothing was not all properly marked? In explanation, I will here state that the first term she went to that school, and boarded in the college building, all her articles of wearing apparel, handkerchiefs, and such things as go into the wash, were plainly marked, as required by the rules of the institution; but this did not protect them. She lost, at that term, three pairs of black woollen stockings, plainly marked "M. L. G." with red woollen yarn; two linen handkerchiefs, plainly marked; one pair high rubbers; one good umbrella; and three dollars in money, — it being all she had at the time. She immediately wrote home to know, or inquire, what she had better do about it. Her mother sent her more money, and replaced the articles lost, and said to her, "If you make a stir about the matter your chum will be suspected, and as she is sent there by the kindness of her friends, and is a poor girl, it may seriously injure her by destroying their confidence; and you had better lose the money." This was in 1861, when she had not the same room-mate as when she left the Hill. Soon after this a dollar's worth of postage-stamps were taken from a book in her trunk. Being postmaster, and having a supply of stamps, I thought best to furnish her with a sufficient number to last her through the term. The money and stamps were lost in the early part of the term. Louise did not think it was her chum that took the money or stamps. At the close of this term I carried my second daughter, Estelle, down to the closing exhibition. On the way down she purchased a pair of long mitts, for which she paid a dollar. Leaving them in Louise's room while she went to a meal, on returning she found they had disappeared. She never found them. She lost, also, at that time, a black veil there.

During her second term Louise lost some small articles, such as handkerchiefs and towels, and one plainly marked chemise. Third term she lost one pair lace under-sleeves, one flannel under-skirt, marked, and two marked nightcaps. Fourth term: one pair sandal rubbers, new that term. Fifth term: one pair marked ruffled drawers, some napkins, and a handkerchief. Sixth term: one pair of spotted muslin under-sleeves, three pairs of white woollen stockings, — all she had, and all plainly marked. Seventh term: one veil, some napkins, and other small articles. Eighth term: she lost one new cotton skirt, marked on the inside of the binding, one wide red silk scarf. And, in fact, at every term when she boarded in the college building, she lost more or less of such articles as napkins, towels, handkerchiefs, veils, gloves, drawers, stockings, etc., etc. Marking appeared not to protect her against loss, nor prevent articles from mysteriously disappearing. In this condition of things, was it any wonder that we should become remiss or careless about seeing that every article was "plainly marked"? And was our daughter alone guilty and censurable for such neglect, when other students, and even her teacher, one of the faculty, could go into her room, and, without hesitation or apology, claim and take unmarked articles therefrom which came from the unmarked pile sent to the wash?

Louise's mother would sometimes upbraid her for meeting with so many losses. She would reply, "Am I to blame for these losses? I put these articles into the wash. They were lost there, and not returned to me. Some of them may yet turn up. We do sometimes get them, after a long while."

The high price of board at the college, and the annoyance of losing clothing in the manner I have just stated, induced me, in the fall of 1865, (being Louise's thirteenth term) to hire a room in Mr. A. Packard's house, where Louise and her two sisters set up house-keeping, so far as to board themselves, while attending school. While they boarded themselves in this house, which was through Louise's thirteenth and fourteenth terms, they hired a lady to wash for them, and every article was returned to them correctly. There was no more trouble about losing clothing until Louise went back to the college building to board, in March, 1866. This was her fifteenth and last term at this school, and she was to have graduated at the close of this term. As soon as she came in contact with this loose practice of mixing unmarked articles of clothing, she began to lose again both marked and unmarked articles. She went to board in the college just eleven weeks before she was sent away, or "advised to leave," on the 23d of May, 1866. Had she continued to board with her sister in the Packard house (which had been purchased by Dr. T.) through this her last term, I have no doubt she would have graduated, and would have been now living. I charged Dr. T., in that faculty meeting to which I have before alluded, with permitting a practice in its nature demoralizing to the young, by allowing the rule, of having articles for the wash "plainly marked," to be disregarded; that it had a tendency to lead them to dishonesty. I now repeat the charge, and will explain how I found matters connected with the washing business, or laundry, and leave the public to judge whether I was, and am, right. The disposition of articles of clothing washed and ironed I found to be in this wise: — All marked articles, sent down to be washed by two girls who occupy a certain room, — for example, we will say No. 20, — are washed, ironed, and put into a box by the side of the room marked No. 20, corresponding with the number of the room from which they came. But if there were unmarked articles, they could not be so put into the right boxes, as the person who irons them could not possibly tell where they belonged, but they were thrown in a pile on a large table.

Thus the unmarked clothing of sixty girls, more or less, from about thirty-three rooms, would make a very large pile, from which, at the usual time, the girls came in and hastily selected such articles as they thought were their own. There was no person to see to the delivery of them; so said Mrs Dagget, the matron, who showed us the condition of things, and told us that there was a great pile of unmarked articles of various descriptions, from the smallest to the largest, which came from the rooms of these sixty female students, and were deposited on this table; and that the girls came in squads, or singly, and after taking their marked articles from the boxes, if they had any that were unmarked, or if, by mistake, some that were dimly or unplainly marked had got on to the table with the unmarked ones, they went sometimes in a lively mood and in a hurly-burly hastily and thoughtlessly selected from the pile, as before stated, there being no one to look after and deliver the clothing. In this state of things, I would ask, would not many mistakes be very likely to occur? Would it not be very easy for any one, who should feel disposed so to do, to say, "I have lost such and such articles," — whether they have or not, — and take from this common pile articles not their own, as it is known to all that nobody is responsible for such unmarked clothing? Those who wash and iron fully understand that they cannot be held responsible for the return of this amount of unmarked ladies' clothing, of every description. Was it strange
 ⁻ʾuise's clothing should get mixed up with others', and that for arti-

cles she had lost in the wash she should take others to wear, until her own should "turn up"? However wrong it might be, it was a practice, as it appears, that was indulged to some considerable extent at that institution.

In my judgment the faculty are censurable for this palpable disregard of this their printed standing rule. It was, as I told them in the faculty meeting, demoralizing to the young, and alike tempting to students and those who had the care of, or access to, the laundry, to allow such a practice to exist. It would have been very easy to have said to the laundress. "Return every unmarked article to the room from whence it came, unwashed;" or, "Return the bundles containing such articles, and say to those to whom they belong, 'Nothing will be washed, until the well-known rule of the school is complied with.'" Had this been done, my child, I believe, would have been this day living. Who is responsible for her fate? Why should the "sin of omission" be passed over in silence, while the act to which it directly leads is dealt with without mercy, palliation, or forbearance?

The reason of Louise's leaving self-boarding at the Packard house, and going to the college building, was that the rest of her class seven in number, were all going there to board through this their last term, and it was deemed advisable, by her and us, that she should go with them. She did go directly from the Packard house to the college, the same day that I took Estelle, her eldest sister, home. Estelle helped her pick up her clothing, and other things, to take to the college, thereby knowing what she had to take with her there.

In two weeks after Louise went to the college building to board, her mother went down to carry our third daughter, Chestina, to the school, and to the same room to board which L. and E. had occupied the previous term. She carried also articles of clothing to Louise. In about seven weeks Mrs. Greene went to Kent's Hill again, to carry provisions to the self-boarder and clothes and money to both. At this time L. remarked to her mother that she and others were losing things in the wash worse than ever, and named several articles she had lost. This was about ten days before L. left the Hill. When Mrs. G. arrived at the Hill, on this visit, she found that L. had not been up much through the day, and complained of her head, and said "she had experienced much severe pain in her head, — had strange sensations in her eyes and head, and was afraid her head would be in as bad a condition as it was some years ago," before she came to Kent's Hill. Some seven or eight years previously L. was so severely afflicted with neuralgia, as to incapacitate her for much physical or mental labor, and it prevented her from attending the town schools, much of the time, for nearly two years, — her head, especially, being much disordered. In a conversation with her mother, at the time I have alluded to, being the last time they ever saw each other, she said, "I feel so tired that I think, after I get through here, I shall want to sleep all summer."

An old student, who had not attended school at that institution for about a year, writes me, and says: "I saw her a short time before her death, and she seemed to be considerably worn out by hard study. I think if the thing could have been kept quiet, and she allowed to graduate, the offence would not have been atoned for by her life."

Before her return home, Mrs. G. went with L. to Lewiston to make various purchases preparatory for exhibition, and other purposes. On returning to the Hill, Mrs. G. found that L. was much worn and tired out. The fatigue and many demands on her, — the much she had to do and attend to, — her studies, composition, exhibition-piece to write and prepare to read on the stage, — the excitement as the time of graduation was drawing near, — how she should appear, and how succeed, — all combined, wrought heavily upon her tired and worn constitution, and overtaxed mind, which had endured the pressure, the wear and tear of five years of close mental labor. A constant and terrible fear, which had troubled her mind for two years, — that the prejudice, which she conceived had existed against her, in the minds of a portion of the faculty, and with Dr. T. in particular, would be brought to bear, and tell against her, to prevent her from graduating, — now haunted her with renewed intensity, as the time drew near. She seemed to have a presentiment that she should never graduate, and often expressed it. All these things had operated, with her physical weakness, nervous temperament, and sensitive nature, to nearly dethrone reason; so much so, that when Mrs. G. left her, only nine days before L. left the Hill, she caught hold of her mother's dress, and made a singular and wild request, of which Mrs. G. informed me when she returned home.

In writing to me, another old student says: "I went to Lewiston at the time she and her mother did. I noticed that she was remarkably still; that is, did not appear so cheerful as she was wont. I had been *well* acquainted with her for some four years. I have no doubt in my mind that she was not herself at the time. I have thought all the time that she studied so hard as to affect her mind."

I have named these circumstances, that the public can judge whether L. was in a condition of mind to endure the severe and heartless ordeal through which, with no mother or earthly friend on whom to lean, she was forced to pass; and to see if the heart of charity among my readers can find nothing that will plead in extenuation of the guilt of that act, committed only a few days after the period to which I have alluded. They will also explain the condition of L.'s mind, and why she said to Miss Case, when she and Mrs. Daggett were ransacking Chestina's and Miss Reed's room, to see if they could not find more articles that others would claim, "I feel so strange! I wish I could think; but I can't."

These expressions were made after this Christian lady had so well succeeded in impressing upon the mind of her old pupil, whose "character had hitherto been irreproachable," the "enormity of her crime." These circumstances, before named, will show whether L. was a fit subject, at that time, upon whom that cold-hearted yet fluent lady ought to have exercised her power of language, further to confuse and distract her mind. And they likewise show why L. said in that memorable class-letter: "I think, maybe I am not exactly as I used to be, while I write this, for my head whirls, and I cannot seem to think, — to say what I am trying to say;" and also in her last letter to her sister: "If I know myself, it was not the true, real Louise Greene that did this. She was trying to live an honest, womanly life; or, if she was indeed drifting into disgrace, she never realized it." Who will doubt that, under prolonged mental labor, her active and ever sensitive mind had become unbalanced? and that injudicious, indiscreet, and unchristian treatment, and unpardonable neglect, springing from prejudice (as we believe), closed up every avenue of hope for the future in life, and sent this poor, heart-broken, despairing girl into eternity?

The last words she ever wrote in the college, as it appears, were these: "Heart breaking. Dearly beloved, adieu!" These were evidently written directly after the interview with Dr. T., when she was advised "to leave that day."

As I have said something about L.'s fear of the operation or consequences of prejudice, I will now give some of the reasons why she and we knew that prejudice existed against her. It was known to us that a prejudice was growing up between her and Dr. T., in the summer of 1864. As I shall occasionally quote from various letters, and from other writings which she has left, I will here state that when I quote from any letter, or writing, I use the exact language, having the originals before me. She complained to her mother — and her writings show the same complaints — of petty annoyances, of insinuations to her, by Dr. T., that she was not just what he wanted her to be; and of his explaining some petty rule of school, and ridiculing some little acts of students after prayers, etc., in a sarcastic way.

I received a letter from her dated "Kent's Hill, August 28, 1864," in which she says: "I have kept almost all of the little unpleasant things which have troubled me, from you, thinking not best to trouble you with them; but the denial of my reasonable request to go home with May Chapman, who lives less than two miles from the Hill." — May C. had been L.'s room-mate for some time; but on account of some difficulty, her father had decided to take her from this school, and send her to the institution at Westbrook. The difficulty appeared to be like this: Miss Case had asked May to rise for prayers, and she declined. This, with some other intimations from Miss Case, or some of the faculty, which annoyed May, coming to her father's ears, he questioned her relative to the matter. She informed him of the case, and told him she thought Miss C. appeared different towards her after this transaction. Mr. C., after having some sharp talk with Dr. T., took M. home. Louise had written to May that she would come down on Friday, after recitation, and stop with her till Monday morning, as this would be the last opportunity she would have to see her before she went to Westbrook.

Accordingly, M. came up to carry her home with her on Friday, as had been suggested. They both went to Dr. T. together, to get permission for L. to go, she carrying my general, written permit in her hand. They saw Dr. T. on the street. L. made known her request, and he refused to grant it.

They both returned, sorrowfully, to the college, where they saw Miss Robinson, L.'s teacher in painting, and sister to the wife of Dr. T. She asked them if they explained all to Dr. T., and advised L. to go to his house, and ask him again, saying, "I think he will let you go." They both went back to Dr. T., and L. stated the reasons why she desired so much to go just at that time. He had before let her go, and no good reason, seemingly, existed, why he then should refuse her. She named her general good conduct, which he admitted.

I will now further quote from her letter of August 28, 1864: "He gave me no answer," she says; "but turned to May, who had not spoken a word, — she was not then a member of his school, — and asked her questions, implying that she had told her father that Miss Case asked her to rise for prayers, and because she did not do so, she appeared different to her after. May says, 'she did tell her father so, and such was her impression.' T. says, 'it was not so, and that she had no right to judge Miss Case. You must not report such things to hurt the school.' May replies that 'her father had questioned her about these things, and she told him; had not mentioned it to any one else. She did not intend to hurt the school.' 'Well,' T. said, 'you had better see Miss Case about it.' May says, 'I see no necessity,' or something to that effect. Returning to the object for which I came, I said, 'Mr. Torsey, if your decision is final, I submit; but must say I think it is unjust.' He said, 'You have no right to judge my actions.' I knew that, although I had spoken the truth, yet I had better not have said it. Almost crying as I was with the bitter disappointment, I said, 'I beg your pardon, sir, for saying it to you. I spoke before I thought.' He said, '*Hereafter you need not ask any favors. You have prevented the possibility of your ever receiving any.*' I said, 'It is few favors that I have asked; still less I have received.' I was standing in the door. He replied, in a voice full of wrath, '*Miss Greene, you will please leave the house!*' 'Yes, sir,' was all I said to him; and turning to Mrs. Torsey, said, 'Good-night.' I held my temper well, for I was boiling over with rage at that moment. Denied, insulted, and ordered out of his house! I was advised to go home with M., and take the consequence; but I did not. One thing is sure, I did not deserve, nor will I bear, such treatment.

"Please preserve this letter. This isn't the first of his tyrannizing, nor the first insulting words I have borne. I will not bear it any longer. I will leave, although I do not want to give up my course of study. Neither will I be any man's dog for the crumbs that fall from his table. I do not feel greatly indebted to Dr. Torsey. All he has done is to drain father's pockets, and give me what justice demands he should give the meanest student. If I stay here I know the man so well! He has bidden me to expect no favors, and I know that a teacher, watching for a chance, can make school life mighty uncomfortable to anybody without doing any open act of injustice or petty revenge. No matter how careful one is to obey the rules or perform all duties, if he detects the least sign of mental insubordination, his wrath is kindled, and finds vent in acts of petty revenge.

"Dr. T. last winter found a way to give Alice White permission to go to ride to Augusta with Mr. B., to see a mutual lady friend and school-mate. Now that was a direct violation of one of the fundamental rules of school, for a gentleman to take a lady, miles away, out to ride! I don't believe another couple in school could have got permission. But Dr. T. found a way by which he could *consistently* (?) let them go, where he had always refused others; and yet I could not go down with my room-mate, when he did not pretend but what my parents were willing, and no damage could be done to my studies or anything else." She wrote other circumstances in detail connected with her case, and finally said: "I shall leave and go to Westbrook next Tuesday if I don't hear from you by Monday night."

This statement of Louise, made to me, I believe to be true to the letter. She said she would read this letter to T. in my presence, and he would not deny it. To my knowledge, he never sought to impeach her truthfulness in this affair. I now ask the candid reader to pause and reflect. What had my daughter done, in this case, to deserve to be cut off from the possibility of ever receiving any favors at that institution, where she had demeaned herself as a dutiful scholar for three years, and had nearly two years longer to stay? And what had she done that she should be expelled wrathfully from the house of its principal? Stung at an unjust disappointment, without reflection, on the spur of the moment, she gave words to a thought, and that thought was the truth. She immediately, and in respectful language, begged pardon for giving expression to that truth: "I beg your pardon, sir, for saying it to you; I spoke before I thought." Was not this apology sufficient and the petition for absolution respectful enough to insure forgiveness from any Christian heart? Yet she was warned that she need expect no more favors at that institution, if her words, which have never been contradicted, were true. With what fidelity of purpose this position, this threat, was adhered to, let the history of May, 1866, testify and proclaim.

M. Chapman was her old room-mate. They had spent many pleasant hours together, and loved each other. M. was about to leave for a distant school. As it was not infringing upon her studies, L. requested the privilege of spending the next Saturday and Sunday with her old chum, at her quiet home some two miles distant, to which place M. had expressly come with a carriage to carry her. No valid reason existed, or was given, why her request could not be granted. Was it just to deny her? and was this not one favor, at least, less, which she asked, than she had received? After she had been guilty of so small an offence towards Dr. T., and had promptly begged pardon, was the spirit of the Gospel here exercised, and the transgressor forgiven until "seventy times seven," or even until "seven times"? By no means. Pardon was not granted, even for one time, though it was sought with humility.

Let the reader remember that hasty decision, and the penalty awarded, and recollect that the same tribunal, if not the same principles, disposition, and antipathy, survived on Kent's Hill on the fatal twenty-third day of May, 1866. "Does the leopard change his spots, or the Ethiopian his skin?"

To L.'s letter I replied on the same day, as follows: —

"*August* 28, 1864.

"DEAR MARTHA L., — I am sorry to have you leave this school until you finish your course of studies. I never like the idea of change; but I was not made to be domineered over by any one, and am not willing my chil-

dren should be. But you had much better remain on the Hill, as you have just arrived there, than to leave so soon. You will not find everything pleasant at any school. You had better stay, if this difficulty can be adjusted; if not, you will please write me again, and I will advise you further. Mother will copy what I have written to Dr. Torsey, and send it to you.
J. GREENE."

On the same day that I wrote to L., I wrote also to Dr. T., as follows:—

"PROFESSOR TORSEY: Dear Sir,—My daughter has written me, as she says, a correct statement of the interview with you; such, as she says, she will read to you in my presence, and appeal to you for its correctness. Whether she had done right or not, when she asked pardon, I think she did not deserve such a rebuff at your house. You tell her to leave your house, and that 'she is precluded from the possibility of receiving any more favors at this school.' How do you think she feels, with these words continually sounding in her mind, 'You cannot receive any more favors at this school,' with nearly two years before she gets through her studies under you, and with the feelings she must now have towards you? Her school-days are made so unpleasant by your ungentlemanly treatment at your house, that, unless some reconciliation can be had, she will leave your school, and that immediately. As much as she and I regret her loss or disappointment, at not graduating at your college, I will not advise her to remain.

"No man, in this free and enlightened land, can unjustly domineer over my children with impunity. I believe she intended to be governed by the rules of your school. No complaint from the faculty has come to my knowledge but what she stood as well as the average of students, in all respects, as to studies and promptness in duties assigned her.

"I exceedingly regret the necessity of this communication. I have written her, that if no reconciliation or adjustment be had, she might leave your institution. Yours respectfully,
"JONAS GREENE."

When I wrote this letter I was not aware — nor am I now — that his dignity or position forbade or precluded me from speaking, plainly and in earnest, to Dr. T., as I would to any other man; or that there was anything improper in so doing. Nor will I now say that hidden motives of vengeance, after slumbering for months, sprang to life and exercise, to accelerate, for this freedom, a joint penalty, at the first favorable opportunity, on her and me. Dr. T. replied to my letter August 29, 1864, in his smooth

4

manner, excusing himself, but not denying anything that L. had written me. He said "he had given her permission to go to the Corner once, on a visit, and once she went without permission." Among other things, he said that her unladylike manner of saying that "he had done her injustice," or words to that effect, and "the manner and tone of her asking pardon, was not satisfactory to him." He also said, "I suppose she cannot leave the school, and her name stand fair on our record;" closing his letter with an insinuation against L., but not specifying anything. The reader will notice his attempt or threat, thus early, to disgrace her on their records, if she left the school, probably by putting some mark against her name; such as "Left under censure," or something of the kind. This threat in his letter to me accounts, or explains the cause, for her language in her next letter to me, wherein she says: "I shall not leave in disgrace. No doubt he would like to, but how can he have me expelled? Where is the act which he can fasten an expulsion upon? But if I *stay here*, that is what I fear."

The misdemeanor of going to the Corner "without permission," of which Dr. T. complained, as L. afterwards explained to her mother, was perpetrated in the manner following: Louise and another student were going down to the Corner (Readfield Corner) on a brief visit. Being in a hurry, L. said to her school-mate: "When you get permission to go, get the same for me." (They could get such permit from Dr. T., or any one of the teachers; but after being refused by any one of them, they were not allowed to go to any other one for the same thing.) The other girl forgot, in her haste, to ask permission for either. So both went without a permit. On their return Dr. T. called them to account, they being together at the time of the interview. The other young lady says: "I forgot to ask permission." L., seeing then how the case stood, says: "If that be so, I am in the same condition. I thought you got permission for us both." Dr. T. says to the other lady: "I will overlook it in you; but, Miss Greene, I shall remember it in you."

Louise wrote me again Sept. 5, 1864; from which letter I make the following extracts: —

"I carried your letter to Torsey. He was non-committal, saying but little either way. But one thing he must do, — take back or modify this saying: 'Hereafter you need expect no more favors of me or the school.' I think he would have granted the request, if May Chapman and her family had been 'all right on the goose' (they were Universalists, as I then understood them), and if I had been one of the Torsey worshippers. I told Miss Robinson, that Dr. Torsey wanted to be to Kent's Hill, what

God is to the universe. No matter how well one tries to do, if he sees the least mental insubordination, he is down on them. I see clearly enough how I could be one of his favorites. Consider his wishes law, his decisions perfect, — let him act for you, think for you, and own you soul and body, and lo! your path up the hill of science is smooth as a gravelled walk. There was a time when I would have striven for Dr. T.'s friendship; but now, I would not take it as a free gift, — all I ask, is justice at his hand. All I grant him, is those rights, which every teacher is authorized to demand.

"If I go home now, I am sure I shall not leave in disgrace. No doubt he would like to, but how can he have me expelled? What rule have I broken? What evil influence have I exerted? Where is the act which he can fasten an expulsion upon? But if I *stay here*, that is what I fear. With a desire for revenge, and dislike for me as motive, won't he find something in the course of two years that will pass for a reason why I shall be sent home, or at least reprimanded publicly? I leave this question for you to think of. It has been an important one with me."

Reader, say you that she had no foundation for those fears, save delusion or vague imagination? and that she did not " discern the signs of the times," and comprehend the disposition, power, and means of those, who measurably held her destiny in their hands? If so, and she had discovered nothing to arouse apprehension and fear, was it not singular, that an occurrence so sad, corresponding so nearly with her expressed fears, should have transpired within the time she specified? I have been censured, and I now deeply regret that I did not give more attention to her request to leave the school. May God and her angel forgive me for the unintentional mistake! Mine was an act of supposed kindness and affection, not of caprice, prejudice, or revenge. Had I then known, as I now know, the many petty annoyances she so quietly endured of the " pimps and spies " that were around her, to report every little act, every " dislike " of which she was suspected (" mental subordination " I believe they call it), I certainly should have taken her away.

It will be noticed that she says in her letter to me, "one thing he must do, take back, or modify this saying : " Hereafter you need expect no favors," etc. As the matter was dropped, or as I heard no more about it, I supposed he did modify, or take it back. I supposed they fixed it up in some way, but how I never knew.

I will now invite attention to some of these annoyances and petty complaints which my daughter endured, and to which I have alluded. The reader will please hear her, and allow her, though dead, to tell her own story. If she had acted the hypocrite, so far as to have impressed upon the mind of Dr. T. the idea that she "was with them," I have no doubt it would have saved her the annoyance of the following described lecture, or of being made the subject of so long a string of complaints. On leaves of memoranda in the last part of her 1865 diary, under date of April 11th, I find the following: —

"Dr. Torsey, in Miss Robinson's room, said, 'he came to me, not on account of particular violation of rules, but because it was the general impression among the faculty, that I was not with them, heart and soul. Marks had come to him, chiefly for being out of room, and light burning. It was not so much *that;* but, so general an impression among so many teachers that I was not with them, must have some foundation.' Said 'Mr. Daggett told him my influence in the school was not good.' Must see Mr. Daggett. I guess he meant that hateful whispering morning. Said, 'Some one told Mr. Daggett that I laughed while he was talking.' (I think the question should be, not 'Did I laugh?' but, 'Did I try to keep from laughing?' if he considers motives so all powerful.) Mentioned class, and said, 'A gentleman told him he was provoked, after the remark I made at prayers, — "darned fool" — to see me in class.' He said, 'some said, I went to gain the regard of a certain young gentleman.' I told him, 'I thought religious matters concerned *me alone.*' I told him, 'he would find, by inquiry, that I had made it a rule to attend one class-meeting, at least, every term,' and I have done so. He said, 'the teachers thought I was one who would lead others into mischief, and keep out of it myself. There would be a great hubbub in the chapel, among the girls, and I would be found looking in at the door.' I told him, 'when I was suspected, they need only ask, and they could know how far I was concerned. I never lied myself out of a scrape yet.' He asked me if I was willing to apologize for saying 'darned fool?' Told him, 'Yes.' He asked 'if I would apologize to those to whom I said it?' I said, 'Yes, if he would tell me who they were.' And there I had him; for that would come pretty near telling where he got his information.

"Dr. T. said, 'Student had voluntarily told him these little things. He had asked Mrs. Brownell about me, and she said, she had seen me standing, — did not know how long, but less than fifteen minutes, — talking with a gentleman on the side-walk;' which looked as though I was coming as near to breaking a rule as I could, and not do it. He asked Mr. Daggett, and he said, 'I was giving him trouble, more by influencing others, than by actual misdeed.' He said, 'He thought it his duty to tell me, if I did anything that looked like a wilful violation of rule, I could expect little forbearance from the faculty.' I told him, 'I had felt that ever since last fall;'—(the turning her out of his house, etc.,—I suppose she meant),—'and had been careful accordingly.' In conclusion, he said, 'Well, Louise, what can we do about this?' 'What do you wish me to do?' I said. 'I want you to begin anew, and from the very bottom of your heart, say, I will faithfully endeavor to obey the rules of the institution.' 'I did that last fall, and I will continue to do it,' I said; 'but I do not feel very much encouraged at your opinion of my efforts,' I added. He mentioned Professor Perley again,—about what he said I said at West Peru. I said, 'If there is anything I can do or say, if you will write yourself, or want me to write to anybody concerning that, you have only to say it, and it shall be done.' Then he said, 'It is not so much these little things; but the source from which they come must be pure,—the original intention right.' I said, 'I don't know what you mean by that.' I must ask Professor Robinson if he feels fully satisfied about what I said about going down to the Corner; as Dr. T. said to-day he did not. I have written fully, and as much as I could verbatim, as I may have occasion to remember what was said."

Perhaps I should here explain, that Mrs. Brownell, here named, was the wife of Mr. Brownell, who was at that time one of the faculty. They were not there at the time L. left; and it would seem as if she was watching to see if any of the young ladies violated this fifteen minutes' rule of talking with gentlemen on the street. Mrs. B. did not say how long, but less than fifteen minutes, she saw her talking. Having seen in this record of Louise what Torsey said, that Daggett complained to T. about Louise giving him trouble, I, Nov. 8, 1866, asked Mr. D. if Louise had been giving him trouble by violation of rules, and that he had reported her to T.? He said, "he did not recollect that he had." Said, "he had nothing to do with the rules of government of students; only oversaw the boarding department. He did not know that she gave him any particular trouble, anything more than being a little noisy at the table." Said, "I spoke to her once or twice at the table." I said, "What was she doing?" "Talking and laughing," he said. I said, "Anything more than having a lively talk and laugh?" He said, "that was all." I have in every possible way tried to ascertain if there was any good reason for his complaints against her "little things," as he said students had told him, and others had reported or complained to him about; and I find that they are small things, mostly without foundation, which looks more like his seeking (asking Mrs. Brownell, etc.) for some pretence to annoy and find fault with her, because of his prejudice, and their conclusions that she was not "heart and soul with them."

Several times, to her mother, L. mentioned Dr. T. with a dislike, a fear, and a terrible foreboding of evil.

What was the occasion, reason, object, or necessity of this visit or interview, and lecture, at the room of Miss Robinson? Of this telling what Mr. L. had said, — what Prof. Perley had told that L. had said at W. Peru? What Prof. Robinson was not satisfied with, and what some one had said about her going to class-meeting to gain the regard of a certain gentleman? No pretension was made that she had violated any rule. Why, then, this threat, that "if she did anything that *looked* like a wilful violation of rules, she could expect little forbearance from the faculty"? The gist of all the complaints appears to be that there was a "general impression among the faculty" that she "was not with them heart and soul." In the pursuit of knowledge, in every department of her studies, L. lacked no ambition or diligence to excel. Her assiduity insured her a laudable proficiency and progress. Her moral character, as Dr. T. himself has said, was "irreproachable." She was ever ready to assist and encourage, by words and examples, those who were seeking knowledge and trying to do right, as I shall show by the best of testimony hereafter. She was not, at the time of this lecture, amenable for the "violation of rules," by Dr. T.'s own statement. In what respect, then, was she not with the faculty? And what was that "influence," rather than "misdeeds," of which they complained? Was she not, with fidelity and zeal, attending to those grand purposes for which such literary institutions ought to be established, irrespective of the creeds or tenets of others? Louise, no doubt, comprehended the variance, and why she was not considered "with them, heart and soul," when she told Dr. T. she "thought religious matters concerned her alone;" meaning, without doubt, that in her own religious acts and duties she claimed freedom, and the exercise of her own opinion.

No doubt she understood the drift of such lectures, when she spoke of letting others "think for you, and own your soul and body." I charged him, in the faculty meeting, with trying to make a hypocrite of her. He showed temper, and said, "Do you say we tried to influence her in religious matters?" I told him, in substance, that I could not say, by direct language, he did so, but the old proverb said, "Actions speak louder than words."

I named to him about calling her to account three times for exercising the right of opinion, in the matter of what Prof. Perley said was told him that L. said at West Peru, when she was home at vacation, — which was merely this: that "self-boarders were not thought so well of, at the Hill, as those who boarded at the college building." We told him that if she said so she said what was true; and I asked him what he desired her to do, but hypocritically or falsely to say what she did not believe. He said, "there was a discrepancy between what Perley said was told him and what L. told him she said." In the whole I considered it a mean, contemptible affair, thus to lend an open and ready ear to tale-bearers, and continue to harass and annoy a student with such lectures. I have evidence to show much about that matter, if I deemed it necessary. Three times, in the course of two years or more (when, as it appears, he had exhausted all other sources of complaints), he would call this up, a mere hearsay from third parties.

The offence of saying "Darned fool," in a whisper, for which she was asked to apologize, and which she expressed her willingness to do, L. explained to her mother, and in her memoranda, as follows: "That after prayers Dr. T., as he was accustomed to do, began to lecture the students for some offence committed by some of the boys, telling what had happened, or what had been told him, and indulging in ridicule in an undignified manner, as it seemed to her, and in such a style of clownish buffoonery that she felt disgusted. That, while his favorites would laugh, as that seemed to please him, many of the best of his students looked upon his efforts in that direction with contempt. That, not controlling her own feelings at that moment, she said in a whisper, not addressing any one, 'Darned fool.' Some one interested to keep Dr. T. 'well posted' overheard her, and went and informed him." It is evident that Louise was not alone in her feelings of dissatisfaction at the overbearing principles manifested in the government of that institution, and the tyranny, as she thought, it exercised towards certain students.

I have before me some letters from intelligent students, associates of L., written to her while they were at home during vacation, from which I will make a few extracts. In one I find the following sentiments: "It is not enough that students obey every rule of the school, — that their recitations are excellent, etc.; but they must be completely subjected to his will. They must not question his actions; not even express their opinion of his silly speeches. O Louise! it makes my teeth grit to think I've got to be under his thumb three terms longer. I won't bow down to the golden calf too much, not if twenty diplomas were at stake." In another I find the following: "Among other things about the government of the school, I despise the teachings and the teachers, — at least, some of them, — yet love the girls, and always shall be glad to hear from them. But as to

Professor T. and Miss Case, I shall not attempt to express my contempt for them. Language would fail. When I think of their contemptible course to students I get wrathy,—for they endeavor to make every one a mere nothing,—also a bad character,—save themselves, whom they liken unto gods. I am glad you speak freely your opinions. This afternoon I attended a prayer-meeting, but very different from yours at Kent's Hill. A holy feeling seemed to pervade all. Such mild, sweet expressions! These are meetings one cares to attend voluntarily. *No one questions my motives!* Many of those who were friends of the institution will not be so now."

In a letter to me, of a later date, this same student says: "The government at Kent's Hill is different from that of any school I ever attended or visited. I understand, from several persons who have been teachers for years, that the government is as was practised years ago. It resembles an absolute monarchy, the president being the sovereign. What respect I had for Dr. Torsey vanished at the cruel treatment of your daughter. Every person to whom I have spoken of the unhappy occurrence considers the treatment unjust and inhuman, in not keeping it among the teachers, but spreading it immediately among the scholars. You have all our sympathy in your terrible loss. Even strangers shed tears for you. A professor in one of our schools told me he did not believe there was such an account on record. Words fail to tell you how I feel for you. But remember God has said, 'Vengeance is mine.'"

Several other letters from students to L. are in the same tone, and express the same opinions as above. From facts and circumstances that have been shown, I leave the public to judge whether there had not existed, between L. and Dr. T., a prejudice, some years before, if not cherished up to the time she left. When I charged him with such prejudice at the faculty meeting, he did not deny it, but virtually admitted it by saying that "he and L. had 'made up' about a year before." Some of the students on the Hill knew that such prejudice existed, and one of them, who was there in May, 1866, said, not long since, "It was unfortunate, in this affair, for Dr. Torsey that it was known he was prejudiced." As to the "making up" of which he spoke, I can find no intimation of it in her writings, or anything she has ever told her friends. The history of the interview at Miss R.'s room, which I have quoted entire, appears under date of April 11, 1865, which was a little more than a year before the time Dr. T. made the statement just alluded to. As nothing else, in her letters or writings, appears, relative to any conversation they had with each other touching the matter of variance between them, this interview and lecture must, I think, be the "making up" referred to. I leave for the reader to say how far such insinuations, such opening of old wounds, such renewal of threats as were exhibited at this interview, could be understood to mean reconciliation of differences, dropping old prejudices, and "making up." It is evident from what she said and left in writing that she did not so understand it, but rather as a new attack, a fresh display of active hostility.

I have given my readers a brief view of some of the occurrences that took place, — a few specimens of the treatment L. received, and the disposition manifested towards her prior to the distressing events of May, 1866, in order that they may better understand the condition of things at that time, and the reason of my views and feelings.

I will now pursue the sad rehearsal of what afterwards transpired.

On the 23d day of May, at ten o'clock in the forenoon, Louise took the stage for East Readfield; thence the cars to Lewiston. At twelve o'clock, the same night, my daughter, Chestina, and a young man, Mr. Chandler, arrived at my house, and told us the heart-rending story, — how and why L. left, as told them by Dr. T., Miss Case, and Mrs. Daggett. Miss Case and Mrs. Daggett, the "matron," or steward's wife, were the two persons who went into the first investigation; Mr. Daggett being called in to assist at a later period in the affair. After examination, all was reported to Dr. T. But it is reasonable to presume, he directed the whole movement; or, at least, that he did know, or ought to have known, all about it. Now, as to the result of that investigation, what was the report which these professed lovers of truth, mercy, and Christianity made such haste to publish to the students, to the whole school and community, against one they had known so long? against one they had never suspected before, and whose character hitherto had been irreproachable, and stood as high and fair as their own? What was this report against one who had made a profession of religion, — a sister in Christ, or at least a sister in the common family of mankind? Why were what they discovered as faults or misdeeds exaggerated and spread, as it were, broadcast over the Hill, in less than twenty-four hours after the discovery, and she denied the least mercy or forbearance, or the most flimsy mantle of charity?

Chestina said to me: "They say Louise had her trunk and drawers full of marked and unmarked clothing, not her own." Mr. Chandler, the student who came home with her, said, "That is the report on the Hill; also, that she had taken five dollars, and had confessed it." "It was the general belief on the Hill," he added, "that she was deranged." He also expressed his fears for her safety. Before I close, I will give the reader some more means of judging whether or not this report was fully true; but, whether true or false, what was the necessity of this haste, and what was the disposition and feeling manifested in making it public property so soon?

On receiving notice of these reports, and that L. had so suddenly left the Hill, in her every-day clothing, — not taking her trunk with her, or any clothes, except what she wore; and that she had removed from her person her class ring and all other valuable things, — we felt terribly alarmed as to her fate. Mrs. Greene and I both expressed our fears, and said that the chance was more than even, that she would be dead before I could reach Lewiston. I made all haste to proceed there; and soon Chestina and I were ready to start. She, poor girl, all in tears, solicited the privilege of accompanying me on this sad and afflicting occasion, and sharing with me the grief and anxiety of this undertaking. She had come by team from Kent's Hill to her home, a distance of twenty-five miles, after six o'clock in the evening, and had slept none that night. We arrived at Lewiston, by team, a distance of thirty-five miles, before ten o'clock next morning. There I made diligent search and extraordinary exertions to find or trace my lost daughter, being assisted very kindly by the city marshal of Lewiston, who promptly sent his deputy with his team; who drove hurriedly from one public place to another, to endeavor, if possible, to get some trace of her. Being unsuccessful in Lewiston, we passed over to the Elm House in Auburn, where we found she had been the day before; and where she had there engaged a private room for two hours, which she occupied alone for about four hours. She said nothing to any one, asked for nothing, and kept her face closely veiled when she came in, while coming down from her room, and when she went out. She stopped about ten minutes in the parlor; sitting down, and looking out of the window, keeping her face veiled. The lady of the house, who came into the parlor about the same time, noticed that she had been weeping, that her eyes were red, and that she appeared to be in great trouble. Not a word was spoken by either, and L. soon went slowly out; and was last seen going towards the Lewiston bridge, a little after four o'clock P. M. [My informant thinks about twenty minutes past four.] No persons have ever fully satisfied me that they saw her afterwards. As there were two letters written by her, evidently commenced in the cars while coming from Readfield, — one to her Sister Chestina, the other to her class, — I have no doubt that they were finished in that private room at the Elm House. Finding she could not write intelligibly in the cars, no doubt she sought this private room in which to write out her last communication to earthly friends. These letters were postmarked, "Lewiston, May 24th," as they would have been if put in on the 23d. They would bear the date they left the office. Believing she did go to that office on Lisbon Street, I thought, if she had not left in the cars, it was very likely she was drowned in the canal or river below that office. When the next trains left, both that day and the next, I stationed Chestina at one depot, while I went to Lewiston depot, and rode over to Auburn at every train, to see if L. took any train from thence. Not finding any further satisfactory trace of her, after riding and walking in all directions, we started out to Sabattisville factory, making diligent inquiry all the way to Webster, Wales, Monmouth, and Winthrop, arriving at Kent's Hill on Saturday afternoon, May 25th. We went thither to see if any information respecting L. had reached the Hill; and also for the purpose of getting C.'s trunk of clothing, as she had no change of raiment, all having been left there. We there found the two letters to which I have alluded. As much has been said about these letters, both in private and in public, and as many have manifested a desire to know the exact and whole contents of her class letter, I will now lay before the public an exact transcript of that letter, word for word, and letter for letter.

LETTER TO HER CLASS.

"*At a Way Station, in the cars.*

"For the class. — Schoolmates, — Once my own darlings (for I have no right to claim you now), I would rather die by slow torture than write you this letter. But I feel it a duty. Who wrongs himself, wrongs his friends. God forgive me! but I believe there is no soul on earth that stands nearer the gates of utter despair than mine does at this moment. I have always said, 'A man who will steal will lie, will do anything bad.'

"Perhaps you will feel so; but, oh! do hear my story. *Do not* believe that through all these past years spent with you I have been acting a lie. As I live, I never touched a cent of money that was not my own, except this once. They tried to make me account for all the little things that have been missed through the term; but I could not. I have not had them. A skeleton key, given me years ago, I had, that looked as though I might have used it wrongfully. God knows my heart! I never did. One other thing I did, — I have been in the habit of doing. When I came to the college I brought many unmarked clothes, some of them new ones. When I missed things from the wash, I took others (unmarked ones) from the table, and used them. They put this with that, and altogether it did look bad. But if my own garments had not come by the close of the term,

I should have left these where I got them, — in the wash. Now you know all. My distress is bitter enough; but the shame that I bring upon you, — upon home friends, — I cannot express it. O my darlings! my darlings! I thought the parting would be hard enough two weeks from now; but this — I cannot even call you *mine* now! The greatest favor I can ask is, drop me from your remembrance, and some time — you cannot do it now, I know; but do, won't you, some time forgive me? Forgive me; forget me; pray do! I ask it in the name of all who have sinned and suffered, — in the name of my own bitter anguish, — in the name of all that I have been, or hoped to be, TO you and WITH you. I do not know what tempted me. I went out to Miss Church's room one evening, without any such thought in my heart. She was gone. Her table-drawer was open; her porte-monnaie, open too. Some satan, hidden in my heart, said, Take it; and before I could think, I stood again in 27. When it was done, I would fain have replaced it; but could not without discovery. The only thing I have to be glad of is, that I did not deny when asked. Everything that was asked me I told the truth about, as near as I could in my distracted state of mind. This storm has only been gathering since yesterday. I tried to read my Bible last night, but could not. I don't believe I shall ever pray again, except to say, Father, forgive me. And He will not hear. How, then, can I expect your pardon! If I could have had an opportunity to retrieve the past at the Hill, — if this thing had not been made public property and common talk, — maybe there might have been a future for me, but now — I think maybe I am not exactly as I used to be while I write this; for my head whirls, and I cannot seem to think, — to say what I am trying to say. Did you love me any? Do you love me any now? It seems as though my heart must have some assurance of this, or it will burst; and yet I know it cannot be. I *could not* go to see you this morning; I did not dare; and yet I could have died for one friendly hand-grasp, and thought it happiness to die. Will some of you call Mary Chapman into your room, and read her this? that is, if you think best. What I write here I put into your hands. I am not capable of saying what should be done with it. Decide for me. Act as you would have others do, if it were possible for you to be in this place. I can hear even now the thousand buzzing rumors flying over the Hill. O my God! what am I that I should have been left to do this thing? Dear girls, it may seem presumptuous in me now to ask a favor; but if you only could find it in your hearts to be kind to my sister, — my poor, poor sister, Ches. ;—oh! if I could only prevent her from being punished for my sins, I would bear my own bitterness alone.

"I do not know what will become of me. If I get home, do not do anything with this letter; if not, will you please send it to my mother before term closes. O mother! my mother! If it were your mother, girls, what should you say? what would you do?

"Mr. Schwagerl said to me this morning, one sentence, 'Remember your Saviour.' I have been saying it over all the way here. I thank him for saying that always. Mary Chapman, you tell him so; but I don't know. The Saviour is an iron door, I think, to me,— shut, bolted. I never realized before that my life was drifting into this downward current. I cannot think it was. I came to the top of a great precipice, did I not? and because I had been trying to walk alone on Kent's Hill, I fell. Well if it had destroyed life with character; but it did not.

"I keep writing and writing because I can't say the last word; but I must.

"I have read this over, or tried to, and it is not what I would say. I cannot write more; I cannot write again. I cannot even ask you to write to me. What could you say? I don't want you to.

"My darlings! my darlings! this good-by is a thousand times more bitter than was the laying away of my dead.

"Addies, Lydias, Sarahs, Mary, and Abby,— how good your names look to me! You have all been good to me.
"Good-by.
"LOUISE."

My reader will pause, and reflect. If my daughter had been so wicked a girl as some would have you believe,— had been a thief, one who had by deception worked herself out of such scrapes,— would she have so frankly told the truth, when a denial might have saved her? Would she have said in that class letter,— would she, when she saw her disgrace and fall in the wretched light she did, have said: "The only thing I have to be glad of is, that I did not deny when asked"— and further said, "I had been trying to walk alone on Kent's Hill; I fell. Well if it had destroyed life with character; but it did not"?— preferring death to the disgrace of this small act of taking five dollars. She writes to her sister that this is the only thing that she feels herself guilty of. She further says: "If I could have had an opportunity to retrieve the past at the Hill. If this thing had not been made public property, and common talk, maybe there might have been a future for me; but now,"— you see her feeling when she says "but now,"— "when T. tells me that the school know of it, when it is so public, and I have no chance to retrieve the past at the Hill, death is craved." Do you believe she thought they had done right to thus early publish her confession to the school, and make it "public property, and common talk," and then advise her to leave in disgrace, and thus prevent the possible chance of her doing one act, or having one day to try to retrieve the past at the Hill? Poor child! She knew of his prejudice, and their disposition to make the matter look bad, on the Hill, and also to disgrace her, else they would have kept her confession private; she knew they could have done so.

I do not believe that I shall ever be able while I live to read this letter without shedding tears. And, when I think how that committee of students did so unjustly and unfeelingly quote damaging sentences from this letter, to injure the character of the dead, and wound the feelings of the living, without giving any explanations therein contained, with evident intent to flatter those who were able to defend themselves, without a word in her favor, or a single syllable of regret for the death of an old student, — is more than I can tell, or they will ever be able to satisfactorily explain to me, if selfish motives were not the cause. And if any one will compare the evidence here produced, leaving out all arguments, they will see how little of what they say is a *truth*ful account of this sad affair is left.

One thing further I believe I ought to say, to show her love for, and determination to speak the truth, let the consequences be what they may. The reader will recollect, that, in her recorded account of T.'s lecture to her, April 11, 1865, in answer to his charge, "that there would be a great hubbub in the chapel, and she would be found looking in at the door," she says, "When I am suspected, you only have to ask, to know how far I am concerned. I never have lied myself out of a scrape, yet." And here you see the truth of that statement verified, when asked about the money, although her character, her *all*, was at stake. She, knowing his threat, "if she did anything that looked like a violation of any rule, she could expect but little forbearance from the faculty," with her great fear that something would happen, for which Dr. T. would refuse to let her graduate; he, as she believed him to be, her enemy, and a revengeful one, " or he would not be watching me continually, and finding fault for such little things" (as she told her parent, when speaking of her fear that she should never graduate); yet, with all this, and her great desire to succeed at the exhibition, the crowning point of her ambition, it does not deter her in this awful trial from telling the truth, and not attempting to lie herself out of this trouble, although disgrace and death was the result. As she says in her class letter, "Everything that was asked me I told the truth about, as near as I could in my distracted state of mind."

HER LETTER TO CHESTINA.

"*In the cars, Wednesday, A. M.*

"My much loved but deeply wronged Sister,—In leaving you, as I have, I am sensible that there is in store for you mortification and a share of my disgrace.

"Dr. Torsey informed me this morning that I had better leave to-day; 'not expulsion,' he said, 'we won't call it that, but I advise you to go home.' Practically, it amounts to the same thing, however. How I feel, God only knows; you never can; and my bitterest agony is for the dear ones at home, on whom must fall some share in this disgrace. Satan, or some evil spirit, must have led me into this. If I know myself, it was not the true, real Louise Greene, that did this. She was trying to live an honest, womanly life; or, if she was, indeed, drifting into disgrace, she never realized it. I can feel myself guilty of but one crime,—the taking of five dollars from Miss Church. No other was alleged against me, but the having of those unmarked articles of clothing; and, as I live, I had no intention of stealing them. For every article I took, I had lost one in the wash, and put these on in their stead, expecting, before the term was done, to find my own. There was, in some sort, a necessity for this; for instance:—I came to the college with three or four good, whole drawers, —two pairs of which were new ones,—and to-day, as I ride away, I have none. They were lost in the wash because unmarked. Was it so strange that I should put on others, also unmarked, in their stead? I tell you this, that you may know what I have done, and why I did it. That five dollars is a mystery to me. I went on an errand into Miss Church's room; in her stand drawer laid a partly open porte-monnaie. What possessed me to take the money I do not know; but I took it out. The moment they asked me about it I confessed it. You know the skeleton key I have long had. That told against me; but, after all, I do not think they believed I opened rooms with it, for the purpose of taking out things. I certainly never did. Now you know the whole story. It is probably travelling the Hill at this moment with a thousand exaggerations. God pity me! I never thought to come to this. Do not tell any one anything in this. It will be useless to try to stem the tide; bend beneath it, or it will break you down. Say nothing of excuse or palliation. In my heart I feel that you will not say aught of condemnation. It is a great deal to ask; perhaps you cannot do it now; but some time will you not try to forgive me? Live down all this. It is no real disgrace to you, though it may seem so. Make friends with the teachers, and with the people of God; they will strengthen you. Here I think was my fault; I tried to stand on the Hill *alone*, and I fell.

"LOUISE."

The reader will notice that near the close of this letter Louise gives her sister this advice: "It will be useless to try to stem the tide" (to try to stem all this prejudice of Dr. Torsey's, — the faculty's whole influence, which is all-powerful on Kent's Hill, — she doubtless meant). "Bend beneath or it will break you down. Say nothing of excuse or palliation;" do not attempt to excuse or defend me; for if you do that, by inference if not by your arguments, you will blame the faculty, and their influence will be brought to bear on you, and "it will break you down." It will operate against you in a thousand ways, to injure, and finally (if you persist to defend me), it will destroy you. This is seen, and may properly be inferred, from this short and hasty advice to her sister: "Say nothing of excuse or palliation." She had tried to walk alone, tried to maintain her right to think and act for herself; but she had found that by so doing she had incurred their displeasure; that her determination so to do, regardless of all his manœuvring and threats, increased his prejudice, and in many ways injured her. She believed Torsey had become an enemy to her. Being so, he had injured her feelings, and troubled her in many ways (not easily explained), although she was right, and ought to have had her right of opinion to act unmolested. Yet she saw that policy dictated a different course; and her trying to "stand alone" on her rights was bad for her, and was the cause which brought down their displeasure "and little forbearance" with her. Then she advises Chestina to avoid that, and make friends with the teachers, — her (Louise's) enemies, their teachers, — and thus try to make "your path up the hill of science smooth as a gravelled walk." "Make friends with the teachers, and with the people of God; they will strengthen you." She does not say she believed her teachers — her accusers and judges — to be such people. She did not mean to say that of Dr. T., I do not believe. "Here I think was my fault. I tried to stand on the Hill *alone*, and I fell."

These letters were heart-rending to me and my distressed family; and it did seem to me that they were enough to draw tears from the eyes of any whose heart was not callous to feelings of sympathy and sensibility, and ought to disarm forever that unforgiving spirit that never seems to realize that "to err is human."

They are a frank and full confession; and by their tone, and succeeding occurrences, it is evident they were intended as her last communication with friends. Her friends believe every word of them was true. The public will judge for themselves whether they were true or false, after reading them carefully, together with such attendant facts and circumstances as will hereafter be produced; and will also judge whether she did or not take too much blame on herself, and feel too keenly this, her first offence, the cause of which she could not comprehend.

As some have referred to these letters to exonerate certain persons in high position from censure, by quoting her confession of guilt, without expressing a word of doubt of her truthfulness on these points, I submit to the reader whether the whole contents of these letters are not equally entitled to credit, as much so as such parts as the designing may select and endorse; and whether those who so quote her confession ought not, in fairness, to give her the benefit of her explanation, and be estopped from denying the truth of such statements as are in her favor.

While at the Hill, picking up Chestina's things, on the 25th of May, Miss Case sought me, and in her cold, icy manner commenced to console me in my sad and severe affliction. Knowing that Louise disliked her, for what I believed were good reasons, and believing she was prejudiced against L., I thought she might have assisted, under such feelings, in injuring my child, and in producing that wretched state of mind in which she was, and which finally destroyed her. I asked her if Dr. Torsey talked hard to L. She said she did not know what Dr. T. said to her. I then squarely asked her this question: "Did you talk harshly to her?" She said, "I tried to impress upon her the enormity of the crime."

She continued, and said that "she was surprised that L. did not feel worse, and break down, as she expected her to do;" said "L. shed no tears, until they opened a little fancy trunk; that she then wept." This is the substance of what was said in that conversation; and "I tried to impress upon her the enormity of the crime," was the exact language used by that cold and unfeeling teacher. Never can I forget, while life lasts, the harsh and cruel course she said she took with my poor bewildered and. distracted girl. That sentence, "I tried to impress," etc., grates upon my ear in memory, when I think of her we loved so well; and I know I am not mistaken in the words and exact language used on that occasion. She, in my opinion, has a large share of accountability, before God and man, for the death of our child. A more cool, unfeeling person I never saw.

This little fancy trunk alluded to would hold only about a quart, and was made and given her by her dearly loved cousin, who died at my house a few years before,— one of the dead alluded to in her letter, where she speaks of "the laying away of my dead." In this little trunk she kept some small mementos of him, and no one was accustomed to open it but herself. This little "keepsake," it seems, could not be exempt from the penetrating search which was made, while they were trying, as she says, "to make her account for all the little things that had been missed through the term."

After dark, Saturday evening, May 25th, Chestina and I started for home, and did not arrive there till daylight on Sunday morning. I found my wife and children in a wretched, distressed condition; for we had neither written, nor brought home any tidings of the dear lost one. Our hearts were nearly broken, being weighed down under the burden of our grief and disappointment.

Although not sleeping any that night, in five hours my almost distracted wife and myself were on our way to Lewiston again. My wife had neither eaten nor drank anything while I had been absent. She looked the picture of anguish and despair. "You do not look as though you were able to go," I said. "I cannot stay at home," she replied. "I cannot stand this awful suspense. I must go." We did go, in a severe and drenching storm of rain. We rode about in Auburn, Lewiston, and Webster; then walked about the river, canals, and streets of Lewiston, inquiring as we went for some trace of our lost child. God only knows our sad and sorrowful walks, our anxiety, our suspense and excitement, until my poor wife was nearly exhausted. I could not prevail on her to retire from the search, and rest, and leave me to continue it without her. She could eat nor sleep but little in such a state of mental anguish and excitement. When all hope of ever finding our daughter had nearly vanished, we started again towards Kent's Hill, to get her trunk, see her diary, and to see if she had not written something and left in her trunk, or clothing, whereby we might get some more light in the matter. We arrived on the Hill at eleven o'clock in the evening, as tired and distressed sufferers, perhaps, as ever visited that Hill. The next morning I called at Dr. Torsey's, and told his wife that Mrs. Greene was on the Hill, and we wanted Dr. T., Miss Case, Mr. Daggett and wife, and as many of the faculty as he chose, to meet us at as early an hour as possible. He called the whole faculty together at his house, and informed us of the place of meeting. We repaired to his sitting-room, and found there present, Dr. Torsey, Professors Robinson, Morse, and Harriman, Miss Robinson, teacher in painting and drawing, Miss Grover, teacher of music, and Miss Case, the preceptress.

I will now state the substance of a portion of the conversation that transpired at that meeting. I may not give the precise language, verbatim, in all cases, but will give the ideas correctly.

I asked Dr. T. why he had not sent for us or let us know about the trouble before L. left. He said "he did not know she was going away." I asked him about what she had done. He said "he knew nothing about the clothing;" but he and Professor Robinson both said something about her having a skeleton key. Dr. T. also told us about her taking the five dollars in money. I asked him "why he had not taken care of her, and sent for us?" He said "she was of age, and he had no authority to do so, or right to control her." (It brought to my mind a passage I have seen in a Book of ancient date: "Am I my brother's keeper?") I said: "You have controlled her by your petty rules for five years. She has been of age for a year past. You could control her while you chose, but when trouble came upon her, you abandoned her."

Having convincing evidence, in my own mind, that Dr. T. was strongly prejudiced against L., and believing that thence an unfavorable influence had extended to other members of the faculty in that direction, I charged him with being prejudiced against her, which he did not deny, but virtually admitted it by saying he and L. had made up about a year ago. I said: "Being prejudiced, you could, perhaps, see little things in her, and call her to account, and annoy her much by your petty rules and your construction of them to her, while you would not notice them in a favorite." In the course of the interview Dr. Torsey said that "L. was all broke down, and wept, and that he himself shed tears; that she said she could not go home, — could not see us, and did not think we would receive her." I then said: "Where, in the name of Heaven, did you think my poor child would go, if she could not go home?" Mrs. Greene said: "Why did you not send her to one of your rooms in your house, to your wife, and let her comfort her?" He replied that she was under censure, and it would not be proper to send her to his wife. (We understood him to mean that it would disgrace Mrs. T.) Then continued Mrs. Greene: "I had rather you would have arrested her as a thief, if it was necessary to do so, in order to keep her, until we could have been sent for." "You would have had no need of that," I added; "if you had only told her she must take a private room with C., and you would look the matter over, and see what was best to be done, she would have done so; and you might then have sent for us before you disclosed to her your intentions." "I told her," said Dr. T., "if she went to Lewiston, she must make arrangements with Chestina about going." "Then you *did* know," said Mrs. G., "that she was *going away.*" He said that "L. said she sometimes went home by the way of Lewiston, or that she would go to Lewiston and write home, or send for us to meet her there." "You must have known her sensitive nature," said Mrs. G., "and the effect so great a disappointment must have upon her. You are an ambitious man, and you would not like to have your character, standing, and high hopes blasted for so small a matter as this five dollars; no, not for five thousand dollars. Do you not think our child's hopes and ambition were not as great as yours? You could not have had her here these past five years and not understand her nature. If you were an ignorant man I could forgive you; but now I cannot forgive you. She had not much money, no trunk nor clothing with her, and she will be looked upon with suspicion at every turn. I do not believe she would be taken in anywhere; and as she left her jewelry and best clothing, when she went away, I think she is dead." As Mrs. G. made these remarks she looked the picture of utter despair. Dr. T. coolly replied: "Mrs. Greene, I think you need have no such fears." Knowing what an old dress L. had worn away, Mrs. G. said: "In two weeks she will be in rags. Where can she be?" "Well," said he, "I think she has gone into some country town. Your daughter in rags, with her open and frank countenance, her lady-like manners, would make friends anywhere; anybody would take her in." "Then she must find different people than you were here," replied Mrs. G. "You thought it would disgrace your wife to take her in for a few hours, until you could send for us." He made no reply. If he had not meant the matter as we understood it, I think he would have explained.

Yes; this (heartless, shall I say?) man could tell my poor and almost distracted wife, in such an hour, and under such circumstances, that strangers would take her child in, while he, who had known her so long and well, and who, we had a right to expect, would be her guardian and protector, at that "safe and pleasant home" promised her, would not take her into his house till we had been notified of the difficulty, which would have required but a few hours, — could not keep her a few hours, it seems, until he could return her to the keeping of the safe hands from which he received her.

As Mrs. Greene was coming down on him rather closely in questions and argument, in order to nonplus her, as it seemed to us, and break her argument and close questionings, he suddenly said: "You have lost a child lately?" Mrs. G. was sitting directly facing him, clad in deep mourning, and he knew all about our losing our youngest child, seven years old, only a few months before, as our two girls were sent for, who were at his school, to go home to the funeral; and he must have known, also, that Mrs. G. took the death of this child extremely hard, and that fears were entertained that her mental powers would give way under the shock. Hence, probably, this attempt to wound her feelings, and divert her from the immediate question, and stop her argument or confuse her, by calling up a subject on which her mind had been severely exercised. Once, in the course of the conversation, he stamped upon the floor, thus trying to stop us and stamp us down in that way. He seemed very anxious to know what we were going to say outside about this affair. Now, kind readers, judge ye: If he would thus try his arbitrary authority on and over us, what would he do and say to our child, if she tried to defend her case?

In the course of the conversation he said: "I told her I would hold her diploma, and if she would live a good and honest life for six months or a year, she could then write me, and I would send it to her." Was it true, then, that he did not *know* she was going away? If so, why did he talk about her writing, and his sending her diploma? She did not feel that she could go home, for she had told him so. Well might I ask him "where, in the name of Heaven, he expected her to go?" Poor child! After five long, tedious years with books and tutors, studying late and early, until her eyes nearly failed her, enduring those hard rides, over rough roads, twenty-five miles, six times every year, in the spring, fall, and winter, and often, too, in cold storms of rain and snow; after putting forth all the energies of her mind to accomplish her studies, stand well in her class, and reach the goal of her ambition, until her physical and mental powers were becoming exhausted by the heavy tax upon them, and knowing how much her parents and friends doted on her, and how anxious they were for her success, — if she could not graduate, which was the crowning point on which her heart was set, but must be sent away, disappointed, heart-broken, and disgraced, — to her distracted mind there was no future for her, and death seemed preferable.

It has been asserted by some, who feel interested to exonerate from blame those who have control of that institution, or are engaged in its management, and the public are asked to believe, that Louise "left the school of her own accord;" that "no intimation was given her that she must leave, and could not graduate;" and that those under whose charge and care she had been placed, did not know or mistrust that she was not in her right mind, or perfectly sane, when she left.

As these propositions are debatable, and, as I believe sincerely, each and every one of them incorrect and untrue, I will endeavor to show that they are controverted by the tongue and pen of the party most interested to substantiate their truth, and, also, by attendant circumstances.

In a letter to me, dated at Kent's Hill, May 23, 1866, — being the same day L. left, — Dr. T. says: "*She left of her own accord, without my knowl-*

edge." In the conversation to which I have alluded, he said that " L. promised him she would go home, or go to Lewiston and send for me to meet her there." As Mrs. Greene had before said that L. was always a truthful girl from her childhood, he rather sarcastically said, " If she promised, should I not have believed her ? "

Prof. Robinson says, in a letter dated Nov. 12, 1866 : " No intimation was given her that she *must* leave the school ; that she could *not* graduate. Mr. Torsey expressly said to her that if she left, it would not be on account of any action of the faculty, but of her own choice. She, at last, promised Mr. Torsey that she would go home. Mr. T. proposed to procure a carriage for her ; but she said she sometimes went by way of Lewiston, and her father would meet her there ; but whichever way she went *she would let her sister make all the necessary arrangements.* As soon as Mr. T. learned that she had gone, contrary to her promise, he immediately sent a student with the sister to Mr. Greene, to inform him of the circumstances and to urge him to meet L. in Lewiston."

Before closing his letter, he says, " *Such, briefly,* are the facts." As no one was present but Dr. T. and my daughter, at this last interview, when it was said this promise was made, Prof. Robinson must be dependent on Dr. T. for all the knowledge he possessed of these " facts," which he announces with such positive and bold assurance. Was this statement, that " she promised she would go home," or that she would " go to Lewiston and send for her father," true ? Was it a fact that no intimation was given her that she *must* leave ? and that her leaving was a matter of her own choice ? As no eye nor ear but God's witnessed this last interview between Dr. T. and my daughter, I will let their pens answer these questions. In a letter to me, dated May 27, 1866, Dr. T. says : " I had a long conversation with her the morning she left, and urged upon her two things : First, that she go to Jesus with the whole matter, etc. Second, that she *go at once* to her father and mother, telling them all." He does not say that he gave her any intimation that he would overlook or forgive, or that he would do the least thing to help her in her trouble. He further says : " At our parting she gave me *some assurance* that she would do both these things." Again he says : " She named going by the way of Lewiston, or writing you to meet her there ; but did not insist upon it, any further than merely mentioning it." From these statements does the reader discover anything like a promise to do any of these things, as asserted by Prof. R. ? Dr. T. also says, in this same letter : " I wished her to allow me to get a team, and that she and Chestina should go, *at once, home.*" After this he speaks of her "finally agreeing, as he understood it, *to make no arrangements herself, but allow Chestina to make them.*"

In her last letter to her sister, written on that fatal day, Louise says: "Dr. Torsey informed me this morning that I had better leave to-day. 'Not expulsion,' he said, 'we won't call it that, but I advise you to go home.' Practically, it amounts to the same thing, however." Practically, she thought it amounted to the same thing as expulsion, so she said; and do not my readers think the same? Dr. T. wished her to "go at once home," he "urged upon her that she go at once to her parents;" he "advised her to go home;" these are his own words written to me. And she had been too long under his charge to misunderstand what his wishing, urging, and advising practically amounted to. Yet, Dr. T. says, "she left of her own accord, and without his knowledge;" and Prof. Robinson, that "no intimation was given her that she must leave," and that her leaving was a matter of her "own choice." This play on words to disguise real facts, to evade the force of what, in substance, is the truth; this attempt to hide the true intent, designs, and purposes of actions, by using certain words and forms of expression, may succeed in carrying conviction to the minds of some, but, I apprehend, it will not avail before an intelligent public. It matters not with me what particular words were used, or things said, to give my daughter to understand what the real intentions were respecting her. Perhaps she was not told in so many words that she *must* leave the school. She says she was informed that she "had *better* leave." She does not say she was expelled. Dr. T. would not *call* it that; but she was advised to go *home*. How could she graduate after leaving the school, as advised and urged to do? Dr. T. has a great faculty to say or write in such a way that he can put any construction he chooses to the same. He well understands the *art* of intrigue and double-dealing.

"If I could have had an opportunity to retrieve the past at the Hill," etc., she says, in her class letter, "maybe there might have been a future for me." When Dr. Torsey asked her, in that last conversation, what she proposed to do, she replied: "I want this kept from the school, and stay and graduate."

In view of the testimony here adduced, I leave the intelligent reader to judge whether it is a "fact," that she left the Hill without the "knowledge," instigation, "action," or intimation of any of the faculty. "I did not tell Louise she could not graduate," says Dr. T. in a letter to me, dated Oct. 29, 1866. "I told her the trustees voted the diplomas, and I would be her friend in the matter." In this same letter he also says: "I spoke only of any time of her leaving when she had decided to go *home* that day." If this were so, why did he tell us in the faculty meeting that she said she could not go home? that she could not see or meet us? And why does he say she promised to go to Lewiston, and send for me to meet her there? What means the following, from his letter, May 27, 1866? "I wished her to allow me to get a team, and that she and Chestina should go at once home. She thought neither you nor her mother would receive her." This statement does not appear to carry the idea that she had decided to go *home* that day; but the reverse might be inferred, namely, that she could not make up her mind to go home and meet her friends then. Is it at all probable that she sought to leave the institution without graduating, and was seeking, voluntarily, to leave it in disgrace? Dr. T. stated, on the day L. left, that she told him that morning, "If she could not graduate there was no future for her." And when asked what she proposed to do, she replied: "I want it kept from the school and stay and graduate." Will he now pretend that when he advised her to go home, he expected her to return in two weeks and graduate? If so, why was she "urged" and advised to go home? From anything that L. said or wrote, it does not appear — to me at least — that leaving the Hill was of her own seeking, or that she ever said she would go *home*. Why, her whole ambition, for those five long years of study, was to get through with all that was required of her, graduate, and obtain her diploma, and her whole soul and mind was bent on this achievement. Having accomplished this, it was her intention then to obtain a situation in some large institution as a teacher in painting, or some other department.

In the "Boston Journal," a paper taken by the Adelphian Society, of which L. had frequently been Secretary and Treasurer (a student has written me, that all the funds entrusted to her care for a long time were faithfully kept and properly expended by her as an officer of the society), appeared an advertisement for a teacher, at Hartford, Connecticut.

L. had answered that advertisement a short time before she left; and on the second day after she had gone from the Hill, a letter arrived to her address, dated at Hartford, Ct., May 24, 1866, requesting her to meet the Principal of that school, at Hallowell, Me., on the next Saturday, to make the necessary arrangements for her to go there in September following.

This was her great desire, to get through her studies and obtain a situation; and, as soon as possible, to get situations for her sisters also, as music-teachers, etc. She had often told her mother, that as I had spent so much for her, she intended to repay it, or its equivalent, in doing much for the other girls, her younger sisters, — so that she and they might be of some use in the world. This letter was heart-rending to us. It was painful to think that the long anticipated, and much desired opportunity was just ready to be offered her, and she died without the knowledge of it, and that her opportunity to assist her four sisters, for which her ambition and anxious zeal aspired, was lost forever.

It was one reason why we desired to give her a thorough education, that she might help her younger sisters.

To say that she did not desire to stay and graduate is advancing an inconsistent idea, at once at variance with reason, facts, circumstances, and good judgment. She had only two weeks longer to toil and strive, and the long-desired goal would be reached. It vanished in a moment, and to her mental vision her future became a blank forever.

It was this bitter disappointment, in my judgment, that veiled the prospects of the future, distracted more completely her mind, severed her ties to earth, and destroyed her life.

What scathing words were uttered in the enunciation of the consequence and penalty of this alleged misdemeanor, or what representations of the "enormity of her crime" were made to the frenzied brain, to increase delusive ideas, and give a false coloring to life's prospects, if any, God and the actors only know.

On that fatal 23d day of May, she wrote a letter to her sister, and directed it to her, on Kent's Hill. She must well know, that, under the circumstances, Dr. T. would be very likely to see that letter the next day, and, if untrue, would be likely to detect and expose the falsehood.

"Dr. Torsey informed me this morning," she says, "that I had better leave to-day; 'not expulsion,' he said; 'we won't call it that; but I advise you to go home,' etc.

"How I feel God only knows, you never can; and my bitterest agony is for the dear ones at home."

Did she not understand his language, when she says, "practically, it amounts to the same as expulsion"? And did not Dr. T. understand the language as she did? Did he not evidently mean she should so understand it? Had he said, "It is expulsion, but we will not *call* it that," would she have understood it differently from what she did?

I have presented many circumstances, extracts from her writings, etc., to show that a prejudice had grown up against her, which appeared to manifest itself in a disposition to find fault with her for little things, and in threats of "little forbearance," etc., if she should be found guilty of any violation of rules. In view of this condition of things, as they evidently existed in *her* mind, whether the *reader* is so impressed or not,

4

what shadow of hope, or expectation of mercy or forbearance had she at his hand? In her class-letter she says, —

"*If I could have had an opportunity to retrieve the past at the Hill, — if this thing had not been made public property, and common talk, — maybe there might have been a future for me.*"

Who prevented her having " an opportunity to retrieve the past at the Hill?" Who made this thing "public property" and "common talk"?

Dr. T. told her, in that conversation in the morning, that "the school knew it;" which meant and implied, as I understood it, that the school generally knew about the whole matter.

He told M. I. Reed, " that he said this to L. that morning she left;" and Roscoe Smith told me, in the presence of others, that Dr. T. told him, "that in answer to her request to have the affair kept from the school, and she stay and graduate, he told her, 'The school knew it, or most of them.'"

Prof. R., in the letter to which I have before alluded, says, " After as private an investigation as *possible*, Miss Greene acknowledged that she had taken several articles that did not belong to her," etc.

This very private investigation was made on Tuesday, and on Wednesday morning she was told by Dr. T. " that the school knew it;" and about this time, Miss Case told all her class all about it.

It was not her confession that revealed the whole matter to the school; for this was not made to the whole school, which she was told knew it, but to Miss Case, her teacher, and Mr. and Mrs. Daggett, the steward and matron. Yet we are told, and it is published from Kent's Hill, that none of the faculty were responsible for these things being made public property, and common talk so soon.

Mr. Daggett, under date of July 2, 1866, writes me as follows : —

"JONAS GREENE, ESQ.: Dear Sir, — Your letter, inquiring who was present when Louise confessed she took $5, is received; and in answer I will say, Miss Case, Mrs. Daggett, and myself were present."

These were the parties who made the investigation into the whole affair; and Prof. R. says, " It was as private as possible."

Three only knew her confession of taking the money, " the only crime she could feel herself guilty of," as she writes to her sister.

It was a wilful misrepresentation, a *lie*, when he said, or any one says, " It could not have been kept from the school." Louise knew it could have been so kept; and, when Torsey told her " the school knew it," she knew they did not mean to save her from disgrace; they meant to enforce his threat, "that if she did anything that looked like a wilful violation of any rule, she could expect little forbearance from the faculty."

This is a point I make against *them*, and *that* prejudice caused *them* so to act. This is what killed her, broke her heart, and sent her to destruction.

Her confession was made Tuesday afternoon, and early next morning, Dr. T. tells her, "The school knew it." Was it true that this matter had been published to the school of some two hundred students in so brief a time? Or, was he *seeking* to *take* from *her* every prop, every possible ray of hope, that she could stay and graduate? Whatever might have been the motive or design, it looks very much like the consummation of the threat, that "if she did anything that looked like a wilful violation of rule, she could expect but little forbearance from the faculty."

If it were true, that the school did know of the affair in so short a time, in whose power was it to have kept this knowledge from them? Who was to blame or responsible for making it "public property" and "common talk" so soon?

It may be answered, that no one was to blame; that no obligation rested on any one to keep the matter from the knowledge of the school, or from the public. Admit this to be so. Do the features of the case bear the impress of moral kindness and Christian forbearance? When one who "had hitherto borne an irreproachable character" had for the first time been guilty of a wrong act, whether rationally conceived and sanely carried out, or otherwise, and who had frankly and promptly confessed the error, without equivocation or falsehood; ought not her former good character to plead effectually in stay of judgment, and postponement of sentence, till all the causes and circumstances in the case could have been investigated, and till she could have had the benefit of a father's counsel, and a mother's sympathy?

Had my daughter been morally and really guilty of the "mysterious" act of which she was accused, and a thousand times more, I appeal to the public to say, whether I ought not to have been notified before the determination that she should not graduate was made known to her.

"She made," says Mr. Daggett, "an immediate and full confession as to the money, and returned it, not denying a word." Had she not reason to expect some mercy, some sympathy and forbearance, some friendly aid from those who should have been her protectors, to help her through this difficulty, and out of this her first offence? Was her conduct much like a sly and guilty thief? Without the least shadow or particle of evidence against her, on being asked about that five dollars, by Mr. Daggett, she immediately told him where it was, and said she would get it for him, and did so. There was no lying, no equivocation, not the slightest attempt in this affair, on her part, to evade the facts, as is almost invariably the case with thieves.

She says to her sister, "The moment they asked me about it, I confessed it." In what may well be regarded as her last and dying words, she says to her class, "The only thing I have to be glad of is, that I did not deny when asked. Everything that was asked me I told the truth about, as near as I could in my distracted state of mind."

The truth of these statements made by her is confirmed by Mr. D. in his testimony to me, and I have never yet heard that any attempt has been made to controvert them. Yet neither her former good character and standing, nor her frank confession and penitence, helped her on this occasion. Her confession became "public property" and "common talk" ere the earth had performed its daily revolution; and, knowing the condition of things, and what had been said to her, it is no wonder that she said, only the next day after it was made, "It is probably travelling the Hill at this moment, with a thousand exaggerations;" or that she said, "I can hear, even now, the thousand buzzing rumors flying over the Hill." She was "advised to leave that day;" thus being informed, satisfactorily to her mind, that she could not graduate.

Chestina, after L. had left, asked Dr. T. "if she could not have remained and graduated?"

"Well, no," he said; "it would not have been best for her to have gone on the stage; she would be pointed out as the girl that stole." Thus intimating that everybody would know of her misdeed and her confession; and expressing himself, as to manner and time, as though the exhibition with her had transpired at the time the decision was made in her case, and she was made acquainted with it, and "informed she had better leave that day." "It would not have been best," etc., he says; evidently referring to the time when this point was settled with her, and she was in prospect excluded from the stage.

In this condition of my lone child, separated from counsel and friends, what did he expect of her, and what did he intend respecting her? Did he intend to turn her out into the wide world, ashamed, disheartened, disgraced, and distracted, without money and without friends, a lone wanderer to the solitude of the forest and the leafy couch of death? If not, — and God knows I wish not to judge too severely, — and a fatal mistake was unwittingly made, why was not an acknowledgment of the error as frankly made as was a confession and acknowledgment by my lost child? And would not such acknowledgment of mistake appear nobler and more Christianlike than seeking to evade censure by attempting to hide behind the invited, self-sought, self-coined and flattered resolutions or public expressions of subservient, diffident, or favor-seeking students, or behind the ex parte report of an ex parte committee of trustees? Why seek to excuse or palliate a wrong, by exaggerating or harping upon the faults of the dead? Prejudice, when suffered to hold too much sway in the heart, is cruel, uncharitable, and unforgiving. It often blunts human feelings when kindness is really deserved, and gives to the actions of those against whom it is indulged a false coloring. Louise, was once expelled from Dr. T.'s house, — ordered out of doors, for telling him a simple truth, even after she had begged his pardon. Do all his acts, before and since she left, agree with the statements now made, that he "had none but the kindest feeling towards her"?

I propose, now, to introduce to the reader the testimony of M. I. Reed, relative to the matter of L.'s leaving the Hill. I will here state, without fear of contradiction, that Miss Reed is a young lady whose standing in society, morally, intellectually, and religiously, entitles her to confidence and respect. She is a teacher of much practice, and, as a scholar and teacher, takes rank before the public when known, among the first order. Being a lady of great energy of character, she interested herself in behalf of Louise as soon as she left, and thereby became acquainted with some important facts in her case.

AFFIDAVIT OF M. I. REED.

"I, Mira I. Reed, of Roxbury, being of the age of twenty-three years, do depose and say, that I and Chestina S. Greene, who is sister of M. L. Greene, were keeping house, boarding ourselves together in a room in the L part of Dr. Torsey's house, and attending his school on Kent's Hill at the time Louise left, — May 23, 1866. I was well acquainted with her, and have been for a number of years. She was generous, kind-hearted, strictly honest and truthful in all things, so far as I knew her. I never knew or heard a word against her character in any way, until after she left the Hill, May 23. I knew nothing about any trouble until about a quarter past ten, A. M., the day she left, when Eliza Bowers and Sarah Dow, two of Louise's class-mates, came to my room in the college, where I was practising, and said L. had gone home, or to Lewiston. They told me she was accused of stealing; said she had gone in her every-day dress. They were greatly alarmed about her; were crying. I said: 'L. would feel so bad she would kill herself.' Miss Bowers says: 'I fear so. Won't you go and see Dr. T.? I think you will do best with him.' I said I would. On my way up to Dr. Torsey's I met Chestina on the street, and in answer to my inquiries she said she had just found a note saying that she (L.) had gone to Lewiston. She also went to see Miss Case, to ascertain how L. had gone. When she came back, feeling terribly, finding she had taken nothing with her, and had gone in her poorest clothing, she went down and out to find Dr. T. She found him in his stable. She came back in a few moments, and said: 'What can I do? What can I do?' and all in tears, threw herself on the bed. I went on the street, and met Mr. Harriman the stage-driver, who had just returned from the depot, where he had just left L. He said she had bought a ticket for Lewiston. I told him I thought she would kill herself before night. He said 'he thought so.' He shed tears. I asked him 'if he would go to Lewiston after her.' He said, 'I will. I think I can do better than any one else, as I am so well acquainted with her.' I said, 'You and Chestina had better go immediately after her.' He left, as I supposed, to get his team. I said, 'I would get Chestina ready in fifteen minutes.' On returning to our room, I found Chestina still on the bed; told her to get up. She should not lie there; she must get ready to go with Harriman. I got her clothing ready. About this time Dr. T. came to our door, and said 'he wanted to see Ches. alone.' I went out into the adjoining room. He went in. When he came out of our room, I met him at the head of the stairs. I told him I feared she would kill herself before night. He said, 'he had no fears of that.' I cited her going in her poorest clothing. (He stepped back into our room, sat down, and talked a long while.) He said 'that looked like going into the factory to work.' We still arguing the improbability of that, he seemed to think she was running away. We said we did not know how much money she had with her. He said, 'he understood she had fifty dollars sent lately: said something about her having a large letter from home lately. His talk and cool argument did quiet Ches.'s fears considerably; but still she, all the time, wanted to pursue her to Lewiston. This conversation with T. was at, or about, or just before twelve o'clock noon. He left, and then there was a long delay, a terrible suspense, — Ches., again taking on as before. No Harriman came with a team, as I expected at first he would. But, between two and three o'clock, P. M., Torsey came up to our room again, and said that the arrangement was for Chestina to go home and let her father manage it, or do as he thought best; or words to that effect. He says to Chestina, 'You will have no objections to going home with Mr. Chandler, I suppose?' I do not recollect that Ches. made any reply.

She did not object; but I knew she was greatly disappointed that she could not go to Lewiston after her. She said so as soon as he was gone; but, as she had appealed to Dr. T. to know what she had better do, she felt that she must submit to his arrangement. Dr. T., in the first conversation at our room, told us, ' that he had never suspected her, Louise, of any, dishonesty in that direction;' said ' he had a long conversation with her that morning. Louise said, " if she could not graduate, there was no future for her." I asked her what she proposed to do. She said, " I want this kept from the school, and stay and graduate." I said " the school know it;" that she then broke down, crying, and feeling terribly.' I was told that Miss Case told May Chapman, ' she had better not go to Louise that night (May 22d), but leave her alone.' As I understand, she was left alone, and her bed was not tumbled; and it is believed she did not sleep any that night. When Dr. T. told us the arrangement was for her to go home, and that Mr. Chandler would go with her, I or we spoke of going immediately. Dr. T. seemed to be in no hurry, but remarked, ' It would be a pleasant evening to ride in; or they could go up in the evening.' Then there was another long delay, a horrible suspense. I did not study or recite any that day. It was so with Louise's class-mates, and with the school generally, so far as I know or discovered. Why, a terrible commotion was on the Hill: an old, and valuable student — one just ready to graduate — had so suddenly been accused, for the first time in her life, and had so suddenly left, in the way and manner she had, there was a terrible excitement and feeling about the matter; so much so that all who knew her, could, or did not attempt to, do much that day, after it was known she had left. All looked pale, and appeared fearful of the result. The report was, that she had taken a large amount of clothing from the teachers' and students' rooms, — valuable marked and unmarked articles.

"I got all out of patience waiting for the team to come. It did seem as if they never would get started to take Chestina home; but after supper, at, or about six o'clock, they got started with her for home, which is twenty-five miles. Dr. T. was informed that she had taken off her gold sleeve-buttons and class ring soon after she had gone.

"MIRA I. REED."

"STATE OF MAINE.

" *Kennebec, ss., January 26th,* 1867.

" Then the above-named Mira I. Reed personally appeared, and made oath that the foregoing statement by her subscribed is true, according to her best knowledge and belief.

"Before me,

"EMERY O. BEAN, Jus. Peace."

Asking my readers to bear in mind the special points in this statement of Miss Reed, and for the present make their own deductions therefrom I pass to the

AFFIDAVIT OF CHESTINA S. GREENE.

"I, Chestina S. Greene, aged seventeen years, hereby certify that I am sister of M. Louise Greene, and was keeping house with Mira I. Reed, on Kent's Hill, at the time L. left, May 23, 1866. Before noon, on Tuesday, May 22, Miss Case and Mrs. Daggett came up, and went into Dr. Torsey's part of the house first, and then came into our room. Said, 'There have been lately several articles of clothing lost at the college, and we have discovered that your sister has been putting into the wash articles that belong to other persons; and in searching her room and drawers, we found articles marked.' Said 'she had confessed she had taken unmarked articles of clothing, and five dollars in money; and we have come to look to your things. We did not know but what Louise had brought things here.' I showed them all my things, and opened my trunk, boxes, closet, and all; and then they wanted to know if there was not another trunk, — if Louise did not keep a trunk there. I said, 'No.' They seemed to think, or give me to understand, that she had committed a terrible crime in wearing the clothing, as well as taking the money. Gave me to understand that she had in her room, trunk, and drawers a large amount of marked and unmarked clothing, not her own. Louise came up while they were there, and seemed to want them to look into everything, to satisfy them. She asked them if they had told me. L. says to Miss Case, 'I feel so strange! I wish I could think; but I can't.' They found nothing there. Making apologies, they left. She, L., looked very pale. I said, 'What does this mean?' She says, 'They have been losing lots of things at the college this term; and as I put unmarked clothing into the wash last week, they lay all to me. They have searched our room, — all my things. This is what comes of having things unmarked. What shall I do? If this thing gets out into the school, there will be all manner of stories going. What will they not accuse me of?' She repeated, 'What shall I do?' I told her 'I guessed it would not get out any further; the teachers would not say anything about it, and it would pass off.' She said 'she hoped it would.'

She looked sad. She went back to the college, and I heard nothing more until I came home the next day, Wednesday 23d, before noon, from practising music, and found in my room, in Dr. T.'s house, a note on the table, saying, —

"'Ches., tell May I have gone to Lewiston, and if she wants to know, ask Miss Case why.   Signed,   LOUISE.'

"I soon saw Mira I. Reed. She asked me 'if I knew L. had gone.' I was on my way to the college to see Miss Case, to know how she had gone; and when I found out, I hardly knew what to say or do. Came up to our room, and laid down on the bed in tears. I soon went down, and out to the barn, and found Dr. T. in the upper part of his stable. I asked him if he knew where L. had gone? He said, 'I have just learned that she had gone, and supposed she had gone to Lewiston, as she spoke of going there.' Said he had advised and urged her to go home. Said his talk with her was chiefly about asking forgiveness of God and her parents. He said that Louise said, she had always had all the money she had asked for. I asked him if she could not have stayed and graduated. 'Well, no,' he said. 'It would not have been best for her to have gone on the stage. She would have been pointed out to everybody as the girl that stole. I said, 'What is to be done? What can I do?' I told him I was afraid she would go off, and make away with herself. I had been to the college to see Miss Case, with the note in my hand, and asked her if she knew Louise had gone. She said she had just heard so. She grabbed the note from my hand, and read it. She seemed to think it very strange, perfectly incomprehensible. She took me to her room, and talked some time. She seemed to be very cool. She could not understand it all, etc. When I got back, Mira came in, and I went to see T., as before stated. And when I came in again, after I saw Torsey, I threw myself on the bed again. By and by T. came to our room, and said he had been to the college, and found L. had gone in her poorest clothing. She had taken off her gold sleeve-buttons and class ring. Had taken nothing with her but her reticule. I was then frightened about her. Said she would make way with herself. He said, 'Oh, no! I do not fear that.' I said, 'What can I do? I cannot stay here, and do nothing. Hadn't I better go to Lewiston after her?' 'Well, he didn't know.' Said he could, or would get me a team to go to Lewiston, or to go home, if I thought best. I did not know what to do. I went again to the college, to find out more how she went, and what she said, and what she wore; and when I returned I saw B. Harriman, the stage-driver. I asked him what I had better do. He says, 'I do not know what to advise you to do. It will cost some ten or twelve dollars for a team to go to Lewiston, and you might be blamed if you should find her there; or, if she has gone home, your father might blame you; and then if she destroys her life, or goes off, he will blame you. I saw Dr. T. again, and asked his advice. He said, 'It is arranged for you to go home, and have your father see to it, or take charge of the matter, and do as he thinks best. Yes, I think you better do that.' He went to see about a team; and, after a long delay, a team and Mr. Chandler came; and we started at six o'clock at night for home, which was twenty-five miles. Mr. Torsey sent a letter to father by Mr. Chandler; but sent no special word, information, or request by me to any one at home.

"CHESTINA S. GREENE."

"*City of Petersburg and State of Va.*, to wit:

"The above certificate was sworn and subscribed to before me this 16th February, 1867.

"B. I. A. TUTTERWORTH, J. P."

We were told at Lewiston, in less than a week after L. had left, by Mr. Frost, a former student at the Hill, "that he received a letter from a student then attending school on the Hill, the next day after L. left, saying, that when she left, it was the opinion of students there that she was not in her right mind, and that she would commit suicide." He further said, "that with his previous knowledge of the management on the Hill, it was his opinion that the time and manner of her leaving, and the fears of students must have reached Dr. Torsey immediately." All who are acquainted on the Hill are well aware how hard it is for the slightest transaction to transpire on that Hill without his knowledge. His Argus eye is ready to discover the slightest move of every student. I could not take a student away two miles, for only a short time, without his knowledge, and a questioning of that student relative to her whereabouts while she was absent.

It will be observed that both Miss Reed and Chestina became alarmed for the safety of Louise, as soon as they heard she had left. The quick perception of Miss Reed told her in a moment that there was danger in her case; while even Chestina, in her youthful thoughtlessness, perceived the true state of the case at the first glance. The disinterested stage-driver, Mr. Harriman, also came to the same conclusion, as appears from expressions then made, whatever he may now say to the contrary, without waiting for arguments and full explanations. Miss Bowers and Miss Dow were alarmed, wept, and proposed that action should be taken in the matter forthwith, and proposed an appeal to him who from his position should be the one to organize action. Yet the acute acumen of the principal of that institution saw no danger, discovered nothing but an intention to go to the factory, or run away. "Had no fears," but readily adopted the preposterous idea, that she would divest herself of her jewelry, leave all her best clothing behind, and "run away," or go to the factory in her poorest, every-day, soiled apparel! It is true, having "advised" her *to leave*, knowing her state of mind, to pursue or bring her back might seem inconsistent, and be at variance with the feelings of the natural-minded man; but in the light of Christianity and the spirit of the gospel, it is better by far to retract a wrong than to persist in it.

I appeal to the candid reader to say whether, in this case, there does not appear to be either a lack in discernment, a careless indifference, or wilful neglect, as to what the result might be. I do not mean to say that Mr. Harriman, the stage-driver, was prevented from going to Lewiston with Chestina by the advice or directions of any one directly to that point; he might have voluntarily changed his mind in that matter; that he advised with Dr. T. on the subject is evident, from his statement subsequently made to me. There can be no doubt, had he been advised to that course by Dr. Torsey, he would have done as was first suggested by Miss Reed, and agreed to by him. It is clear, to my mind, that it was the management of Dr. T. that prevented his going. Miss Reed, and others, understood that L. was not in a condition of mind to be safely trusted off alone. Were their facilities greater, and their opportunity better, for judging of her state of mind than were Dr. Torsey's? He had had a "*long conversation with her*" that morning, whereas it does not appear that the others had. He must have discovered the despair and despondency that seized upon her mind when she declared "there was no future for her;" that it was sealed up. From passages which I have quoted from both Dr. T.'s and Professor R.'s letters, it appears plainly that L. was not considered sound in mind, or, at least, was under such mental excitement that she was not accounted competent to make arrangements for, and take care of, herself. "Finally agreeing," says Dr. T., "as *I understood it*, to make no arrangements herself, but allow Chestina to make them." What did this mean? What is the inference? "*But she said*," says Professor R. in his letter, "*she sometimes went by the way of Lewiston, and her father would meet her there; but whichever way she went, she would let her sister make all necessary arrangements for it.* As soon as Dr. Torsey learned that she had gone, contrary to her promise, without the knowledge of her sister, he immediately sent a student, with the sister, to Mr. Greene," etc.

Louise was twenty-two years of age, while Chestina was but seventeen. L. had been on the Hill, through the terms, for five years, — was well acquainted, and at home there; while Chestina, comparatively, was but a stranger there. Why was it insisted that this young sister should make all the arrangements? Why did L. make such an agreement or promise, if she did make such as they say, unless it was suggested and urged upon her? Why was she, who "*was of age*," as Dr. T. once told us, and who had formerly acted the matronly part towards that sister, to be placed under her youthful guardianship on this occasion, unless she was considered by him in such a state of mind as to be incompetent to make arrangements for herself? Circumstances show very plainly that it was on account of her "bewildered" and excited state of mind, as manifested by her appearance, and the result shows that in that matter, at least, the conclusion and judgment were correct.

Having shown my readers a portion of the circumstances, and a part of what was said and done to influence or cause the exit of my daughter from the Hill, I will now ask them to go with me farther into an examination of her guilt and crime, in the matters of which she has been accused. I believe, in all well-ordered courts, before any just tribunal, whatever may have been the crime, the culprit is held to be entitled to all the benefit of a previously good character, which, before a humane tribunal, pleads in mitigation of penalties incurred. I have shown, by certificates, the character L. sustained in her own town and in the towns where she had been employed as a teacher. I will now show how her character was understood on Kent's Hill, by those who had the best opportunity to form correct opinions respecting her, and where she had been a sojourner, during the terms, for five years. For this purpose, I will call some of her class-mates, and other students who were school-mates of hers, and let their written statements answer. I will here say that, in quoting and making extracts from letters, I copy from none except from persons who are, or have been, in some way connected with Kent's Hill institution. My motive in withholding signatures for the present will be appreciated and understood, when I state that the position and relation of many of the writers, at present in connection with that institution, might render the publicity of their names unpleasant to them, and make them subject to such annoyances as have sometimes fallen to others. I have now before me a letter, handed me by the clerk of Peru, who says there is no impropriety in my publishing it entire. It is as follows:

"*Winslow, December 16th, 1866.*

"Mr. S. R. Newell: Sir,—Your letter came to hand yesterday, and I was very glad to receive it; for I have long wished for some avenue through which to express my esteem and love for Louise, and inexpressible sorrow for her untimely death. Louise was not only my class-mate, but my very dear and personal friend, for three years. Being such, I could, perhaps, form a better estimate of her character than many others.

"During all the close intimacy of school-girl life, up to the time she left us, her life was not only one of morality, but of unselfish and careful consideration of the happiness of others. Through all our friendship, I never heard her speak evil of any one, except a few times, when her sensitive spirit had been stung to the quick by a careless word let fall by those who considered her destitute of feeling. For the sake of making others happy, she seemed to lay aside all those likes and dislikes so common to school life, and yet so strong while they last.

"She was literally a peace-maker. Many a one can testify to difficulties smoothed and hours made happy by her. Many a one has gone to her in trouble, and, laying aside her own pursuits, she would cheerfully give them her aid, until the trouble was removed.

"She had the rare talent of adapting herself to the company around her, and endeavoring to make the time pass as pleasantly as she could. How often, during some of the 'dark days' which come to all, have I been comforted by our dear Louise! How many happy hours do I owe to her who has gone from us forever! Of her literary acquirements, perhaps I need not speak; they are well known to many students who have attended school with her. Besides the knowledge acquired by study, Louise was naturally very talented; in my estimation as much so as any one who ever went from Kent's Hill during my stay there. Of her death, and the sad cause of it, I can say nothing that would throw new light upon it. Only, in my sorrow, I remember that the Father of all judges not as man judges. I could fill page after page with expressions of the worth and acquirements of our departed Louise; but perhaps I have said enough for every purpose. Accept these few lines as an earnest and sincere tribute to the memory of Louise, from one who knew her intimately, and loved her dearly.

"Yours, etc., Adelaide Webb,

"Class-mate of Miss Louise Greene."

I have also before me a few other letters from her class-mates, handed to me by the same friend. I shall not weary the reader with the perusal of all these letters entire, but shall make such extracts as may seem directly to touch the point now under consideration. In one of these, under date of December 28, 1866, I find the following: —

"I scarcely know what to say to you after my former letter. I was unable to consult the class, we were so far separated, so we might act together.

"I then thought I could as easily speak to the public of Miss Greene, as to you, or any one, in private. But when trying to write for publication, I could not do it, and, for several reasons, think it best not to publish anything. I regarded her character as above reproach, until this last act. This I could say, *but it has* been said continually, to the public. We all know she ought to have been saved; but we, as it were, were paralyzed with grief, and did not *act* as we now regret so much."

From another of these letters, dated Dec. 26, 1866, I make the following extract: —

"No one could have admired or appreciated, more fully than myself, the truly superior talents of our lamented class-mate. No one is more pleased than myself to speak of her beautiful traits of character, or to dwell upon the perfect kindly feeling that ever existed between us, as *friends*, as *class-mates*, as *sisters*, in *class* and in society.

"Of these things I think much; of them I am ever happy to speak to others.

"I feel that anything from my pen for the purpose of publication is uncalled for.

"I feel that in this case public opinion has ever been and now is very charitable and sympathetic, and seems to demand no further proof of the many *talents* and *virtues* of our beloved friend."

I will now give a few extracts from other letters, written by L.'s schoolmates and class-mates to different persons. I copy from a letter dated Nov. 4th, 1866: —

"I think it a fact, that no student has ever been more universally beloved than was Louise. Indeed, I do not know of a single person who bore any feeling of dislike to her; and as long as I have been here at school (five terms), I have never heard a word against her moral character either from teachers or students.

"A year ago last spring she sat next to me in one section in the college dining-hall. I used to like her lively conversation; and as I got better acquainted with her, and learned what a kind, womanly heart she had, I learned to love her, and I used to think she had some love for me."

Another student, writing under date of March 24, 1867, when speaking of being acquainted with L., says:—

"And I knew her but to love and respect; and think I am but expressing the sentiment of her numerous circle of friends and acquaintances when I say, she was universally respected and beloved. Her standing in the school was of the highest rank, and her scholarship and ability unquestioned. I know of none in my whole circle of acquaintance on the Hill, who occupied, in the affections of their school-mates, a position so enviable.

"If others seek to do her injustice, God forgive them!

"Unfortunate as is the past, I cannot censure.

"As a class-mate and personal friend, our acquaintance, though, perhaps, not intimate, was yet sufficient for me to say, in all truth, I believe her to be as free from any intentional wrong as is possible for weak humanity to be. I would write whatever of wrong in sand."

I have before me another letter, written by one of her class-mates, and as it was the young lady to whom her "class letter" was directed, and as confining myself to extracts would in a measure destroy the beauty and pathos of the sentiments therein contained, I will give the letter entire,— a splendid endorsement of her character by one who knew her well, as follows:—

"*Unity, Maine, Sunday, Oct.* 21, 1866.

"Mrs. Greene: Afflicted Parent of 'our Sister,'— As your family assemble to-day, in agonizing grief, to lay away the sacred remains of 'dear Louise' in its last resting-place, near by her own loved home, you cannot know the many mourning hearts that sympathize with you in this your deepest affliction. You cannot see the bitter tears that fall with yours to-day over 'our dear sister's' fate. As I sit alone in my own little room to-day, my thoughts are all with you, my stranger friends, and oh, I fain would fly to you and tell you of my sympathy, and beg you never to forget that we, her 'sisters,' mourn with you this great bereavement,— yours first, ours next. Although I am but one, I know I speak the hearts of all the *class*. Oh! could you have known the agony that rent our hearts, when first we knew 'our sister,' had left us; could you have seen the *sorrow-stricken group* that assembled in my room as *that* precious letter, her last message to us, was received; could you have looked into our hearts, and seen, through these long months, the restless watching for some *trace*, some knowledge, some message from 'our poor Louise,—

and when at last it came, how did the dreadful bolt strike home to every sister heart!—could you but know *all* this, as *I do* know it, you could never doubt our grief, but would feel, if sympathy can lessen grief, or soothe the mourner, that your own heart-crushing agony had lesser grown, and that a soothing balm were falling on your overburdened spirit. Would that I could say some word of consolation; but well I know how vain are words to express what the heart would dictate at such a time. One little thing I wish to mention, my dear stranger friend, and may the simple instance impress you as beautifully as it did myself. Yesterday, my mother and I had been speaking of Louise all the afternoon, — of her brilliant powers of mind; her uncommon talent for writing; her kindness and self-sacrificing regard for her friends; her charity for the faults of others; her encouragement to those who were striving to do right; of our sorrow at her fate so sad, so awful; and our deep sympathy for you in your heart-breaking agony,— of all these things we were speaking, when, as I passed into another room, I picked up a piece of a torn paper that had been accidentally dropped by some one, and my eye fell upon a piece of poetry, entitled, ' Lines to a 'Skeleton,' that seemed so very beautifully appropriate to the occasion, that I really thought it strange. My mother was equally impressed with its beauty; and I cannot refrain from sending it to you, hoping that it may bring to you the same soothing influence that fell upon my heart, as I read it.

"Dear Mrs. Greene, — I have a great favor to ask of you, the granting of which would render me very thankful. That letter that *dear Louise* sent to us — her class — was directed to myself. I remailed it to you, after having reserved a copy for each of us; and also the envelope in which it came, which bears my name (Eliza J. Perley). If 'tis preserved, and you have not the *slightest objection, I* would prize *that simple envelope very highly,* as a last token to myself from *one I loved so dearly;* and oh! if you could send me, too, one of her pictures, I would be very thankful. She had mine, but had none of her own to exchange at the time. I desire one very much. Pardon these requests from one who is a stranger to you; but be this my plea, — *your dear Louise* was *dear* to *me.* *Your daughter* was *my sister.* But now, stranger friend, good-by; and may a *God* of *love* and mercy strengthen your heart in your affliction, is the prayer of

"Eliza Perley."

I think I have produced sufficient testimony to establish the good character of my daughter up to the time when she was first accused of any serious wrong. As no one ever assailed her reputation up to that time, it may seem to some quite needless that I have said so much. But when it is considered that it is contrary to the common course of vice, for any one to plunge at once from the height of seeming virtue to deep infamy and disgrace at the first step, I wish to show my stranger reader, who may infer, from the fact that the act was committed, that her character was previously bad, that there is a mystery here; and if my daughter was rationally and intentionally guilty of the wrong with which she was charged, it is a case at variance with precedent, and the usual progress of iniquity.

I have endeavored to show that the last statement of Louise respecting being advised to leave that day, was true. I propose now to show that her statement concerning the clothing was true, also.

After leaving the faculty meeting, on the 30th day of May, which I have before mentioned, not obtaining much information, from that quarter, relative to the charges brought against L., of taking clothing not her own, and being told by Miss Case that Mrs. Daggett knew best about that matter, we repaired to the college, to have an interview with Mr. and Mrs. D. Dr. Torsey had preceded us thither, probably to report "progress," and look after his own side and interest in the affair. Mr. and Mrs. Daggett did not meet us in the faculty meeting, as was requested by me, perhaps for the reason that it might seem a little beneath their dignity to have their steward and his wife present in their dignified faculty meeting.

We told Mr. Daggett that we had come to learn about the charges against Louise, of taking clothing, etc. He told us he knew but very little about the clothing, as he was not present at that investigation; but referred us to his wife. Dr. Torsey then showed us into Mrs. Daggett's room, where we had a conversation with her relative to the clothing said to have been taken or stolen. The substance and material parts of that conversation will appear in the following

CERTIFICATE OF JONAS GREENE.

"I, Jonas Greene, do hereby testify and declare, that on the 30th day of May, 1866, myself and wife called at the room of Mrs. Daggett, in the college building on Kent's Hill, and said to Mrs. Daggett, 'We have come to know about the charges against our daughter.' Mrs. Daggett said, 'Do you want to know all?' I replied, 'Yes; that is what we have come for.' She said, 'If it will not hurt your feelings, I will tell you all' (speaking as though our feelings could be worse hurt than they already were at the treatment our child had received, when we had then searched a week for her in vain, and believed her dead).

"She then said, 'The first we thought or had any suspicion was, that Louise had been putting cotton drawers, not her own, into the wash, for five or six weeks.'

"'Were they marked?' we asked.

"She answered, 'No.'

"Mrs. Greene and I had agreed, before entering the college building, that if they said any of the things were marked, we would request them to produce the articles, that we might see if they were plainly marked, or if there was not some mistake in the mark, or some chance for a wrong construction to be put upon the real fact.

"Mrs. Daggett continued, and said, 'We entered and searched her room and things while she was at meals, down at the table. We found in her room, trunk, and drawers, some articles that did not belong to her.'

"We asked, 'Were they marked?'

"She answered, 'No.'

"'Do you take the liberty,' we inquired, 'to unlock, enter, and search students' rooms when you please?'

"'Oh, yes,' she replied; 'we could not get along here with so many students without that right, or without doing so.'

"We asked her how she knew that these articles did not belong to Louise. In substance, she replied, that they belonged to some other persons; that 'two collars belonged to Miss Case; that they were new style, tucked linen; and that none in the college, except three teachers, had such collars.'

"'Were they marked?' we asked.

"She answered, 'No.'

"She then said, that 'Louise told her they were lately brought to her by her mother.' She said, 'Miss Case took them.' She said, 'Something was said to Louise about the clothing on Monday night; but they did not go into investigation until Tuesday, May 22d.' She said, that 'she and Miss Case went to Louise, and questioned her, she not knowing that they had been into her room, and searched all her things; that they asked her if she had any articles of clothing in her room, not her own;' that L. replied, 'I think likely there may be.' 'That they then asked her if she had such and such an article,'—naming two. She replied 'Yes; I think so.' 'That they then asked her if she had such an article,'—naming a third in her room. She answered, 'No.' That they then told her the article was in her room, and that she had denied a knowledge of it. That they then showed her the article, and inquired of her whether it was hers. That she said, 'it was not.' We then again asked. 'Was this marked?' Mrs. D. answered, 'No.'

"Mrs. D. represented this to us as L.'s denying a knowledge of the article, and then owning she had stolen it, with other articles, which she owned were in her room.

"She told us about L.'s having an unbleached chemise, which Miss A. Harriman claimed. 'Was that marked?' we asked. She answered, 'No.' She said, 'It was put into the wash the Monday before L. left.' She told us about another chemise, which Miss Case claimed, which was in L.'s room, and which L. said did not belong to her. 'Was this marked?' was our inquiry. 'No.' was her reply.

"A linen handkerchief, which belonged to Carrie Straw, and which L. said was not hers, Mrs. Daggett told us was found in L.'s room. 'Was it marked?' we asked. 'No,' was the answer.

"She then told us about one or two towels being found in L.'s room, one of which L. said was not hers.

"'Were they marked?' was the inquiry; and 'No,' was the answer.

"She also said something about some under-sleeves; but said they were not marked. She said L. put into the wash on Monday, the 21st of May, two days before she left, two weeks' washing, with a *written list* of the articles to be washed, and returned to her and her chum's box. (L. was absent with her mother, at Lewiston, on the Monday previous, on the 14th, and could not put in her week's washing.)

"In this bundle, Mrs. D. said, was the unmarked chemise which Miss Harriman claimed; also, one ruffled chemise, which was taken to Miss J. Sherburn's room, on Monday, to see if she would claim it. She did so. We asked if that was marked. She said, 'No.' She said there was one pair of cotton drawers in the bundle that belonged to Miss Lucy Belcher. 'Were these marked?' we asked. She answered, 'No.'

"By this time we were getting out of all patience, in view of the current reports that had reached us at every turn, that L. had in her room, trunk, and drawers, a large lot of marked, as well as unmarked articles, and we asked if there was anything marked. Mrs. D. said, 'Yes, a linen handkerchief.' Mrs. Greene said, 'Was it a nice one?' 'No,' was her reply.

"'Was it new?' said Mrs. Greene.

"'No,' was the answer.

"'Was it an old one?" continued Mrs. Greene.

"'Yes,' said Mrs. D., 'with holes in it.'

"'Was this all that was marked?' said Mrs. G.

"Mrs. D. said, 'There was a pair of stockings that looked as though a mark had been pulled out.'

"Mrs. Daggett stopped here.

"Mrs. Greene then said, 'How did Miss Case and others know that these articles were theirs?'

"'Oh, by the sewing,' said Mrs. D.; 'and by the quality of the cloth. Could you not tell your girl's clothing?'

"'No,' said Mrs. Greene; 'I could not tell with certainty in that way. Many of her clothes were made out of our house, by others; and I do not believe those who claimed and took those articles, could tell, with any certainty, whether they were theirs or not. No doubt they had lost articles enough, and were glad to get what they could. They might be perfectly honest, and really believe they were theirs.'

"This conversation was just one week after Louise left the Hill, when all the circumstances must have been fresh in the mind of Mrs. Daggett.

"JONAS GREENE."

"*Oxford, ss., August 24th, A.D.* 1867.

"Personally appeared, Jonas Greene, and made oath that the above certificate and statement by him subscribed, is true, as being the substance of the conversation touching the subject therein named.

"Before me,
"ROSCOE H. THOMPSON,
"*Justice of the Peace.*'

"I, Louisa M. Greene, hereby testify that I was present in the room of Mrs. Daggett, on Kent's Hill, on the 30th day of May, 1866, during the conversation alluded to in the certificate of my husband, Jonas Greene, and do know, assert, and declare that the same is true.

"LOUISA M. GREENE."

"*Oxford, ss., August 24th,* 1867.

"Personally appeared the above-named Louisa M. Greene, and made oath that the above statement by her subscribed, is true.

"Before me,
"ROSCOE H. THOMPSON,
"*Justice of the Peace.*"

I appeal to the public, to any profound lawyer or jurist, to say whether they had any evidence on which they could rely, to hold these common white under-garments, when it is a known fact that in nearly all the dry-goods stores in the State may be found the same style and quality of cloth, manufactured at the same mills, and that the manner of making such articles is about the same all over the State. I appeal to them, also, to say whether it was dealing fairly with my daughter to enter her room and take such unmarked articles, passing them through the rooms of the college, to see if they could find any student to claim them, in order to implicate her in taking them; and thus making the matter public in the onset. Does it not look as though having detected L. in a misdemeanor, which she promptly confessed, they desired to make it tell as hard against her as possible, and were willing to arouse suspicion against her, and magnify her faults rather than palliate, — to wound, rather than console, her already distressed and " distracted " mind? Does it not appear, from the manifestation of this disposition, that the last statement of L. was true when she said: " They tried to make me account for all the little things that had been missed through the term "?

I had another interview with Mrs. Daggett, in her room, on the 8th of November, when, at my request, she went over the whole account of accusations against Louise, adding many new statements, and materially altering others. At this time, as well as at the first time we talked with her, she showed evident signs of prejudice, and a willingness to make the whole matter appear as bad as possible against Louise.

Whether these variations in her statements were made on account of her recollections of the affair being more vivid after the expiration of nearly eight months, than in one week after the transaction, or for the purpose of excusing or shielding the faculty, or any one of them, from censure, I leave the reader to judge. And whether her seeming prejudice was real and self-conceived, or instigated by others, and in their interest, is more than I can tell. Dr. T., in a letter to me, dated June 30th, 1866, makes his charges against L. in the following language: —

" The facts, I believe, are these: Louise sent, at different times, bundles of clothing to the wash, from which were taken, by the wash-girl, five articles of clothing not hers. In her room were found nine or ten articles, some of them marked, some of them not, having been sent to the wash, — some of them belonging out of the building. Before they were shown her, she denied she had such articles in her room. The money she took, and put out of her hands at once. For three years she had kept a skeleton key, opening all of the students' rooms." Mark what he says: " The facts, *I believe*, are these." He does not *know* the facts are so. He told us he did not know what the facts were, in the faculty meeting. Miss Case told us the same in that meeting, and Mr. Daggett told me the same May 30th, and November 8th, 1866. Nobody pretended to know but Mrs. D., and nobody does know what the facts were, except Mrs. D. Mrs. D. had told us, or endeavored to tell us, all about this matter of stealing clothing, as they represented it, on the 30th day of May. Time rolled on. Louise was lost, and could not be found. The public began to understand more about this sad affair, and seriously to censure some of the faculty. Public excitement was increasing, and the necessity seemed to exist of making L.'s case as bad, and look as dark, as possible. New discoveries were made of articles in her room, which had evaded the scrutinizing search of Mrs. D. and Miss Case, when they searched everything in her room, even the body of the doomed girl, to her very under-garments on her, as Mrs. D. told me.

I will here say, that it might be a misdemeanor in L. not marking her clothes. If so, she was not alone in the fault, as other students, and even the teachers, were guilty of the same. If it had not been so, Miss Case and others could not have claimed the unmarked articles found with Louise, some of which, no doubt, belonged to her, as I shall hereafter endeavor to show.

As Dr. T., Mrs. Daggett, and others, in their charges against Louise, and in their letters, use the term " her room," it is proper for me to inform the reader that L. did not occupy the room alone, but had a room-mate, who occupied the same bed with her, each furnishing one-half the sheets and pillow-cases. They occupied the room and clothes-closet in common. Their clothes, when washed and ironed, were put in the same box; sometimes one, and sometimes the other, and sometimes both together, going after them. Was there anything mysterious in the matter, that an article was found in the room thus occupied, of which she had no knowledge? And would such finding, and her denial of a knowledge, of such articles furnish sufficient evidence, in the opinion of any sound-minded man, to convict her of stealing, or of any intention to steal?

I have used the term " stealing," not because I do not know, nor because I suppose that every well-informed reader does not know, that this act of " taking clothing," of which they accuse her, is not stealing in the light of the law; but because I have reason to believe, from circumstances, and her last letter to her sister, that they did " impress upon her mind the idea and conviction that they considered her guilty in this matter of stealing the unmarked articles found in her room which were not her own." She says in her letter: " As I live I had no intention of stealing them;" which shows plainly that the same accusation had been made to her which has been reported to the public, — that she stole these articles.

Taking these unmarked articles in lieu of her own, which were gone, which had been taken, perhaps, by others in like manner, might be contrary to the *rules*, if not the *practice*, at the institution, and a misdemeanor or trespass before the law; but to take articles in such a manner, to use and not to keep, in open day, to wear and expose them without concealment, returning them to the wash openly, with a list of the same, and her own signature or name affixed, as she did, in this case, no jurist would pronounce it larceny.

F. A. Robinson, one of the faculty, under date of November 12, 1866, writes as follows : —

" The facts in the case are these : After as private an investigation as possible, Miss Greene acknowledged that she had taken several articles that did not belong to her. Also, that she had taken money from one of the young ladies. Also, that she had had in her possession, for two years, a false key, which would open most all the students' rooms in the college."

He does not say what these articles were, nor how they were taken, but uses the word " taken," evidently intending to be understood " stolen." Neither does he say, as did Dr. T.: " The facts, I believe, are these." It was then November. L.'s remains had been found, and her tongue and pen must be silent forever. From what has already been shown, and the fact that Dr. T. told L. the next morning after the investigation that the students knew of the affair, will the reader call it anything like a " private investigation "? I know that many of the students did not know of the matter the next morning after she confessed ; they have told me so. But did he not mean she should understand that the school knew it when he told her so?

Since writing the statement of a conversation with Mrs. Daggett on the 30th day of May, 1866, a copy of a written statement made by her, as also one made by Mr. D., has fallen into my hands. Presuming that these statements were intended to correct the opinion and relieve the mind of the person to whom they were addressed of the impression that injustice had been done to Louise, by placing before him, over their own signatures, the extent and magnitude of her offences, I will give them the benefit of these productions by laying them entire before the public.

COPY OF MRS. DAGGETT'S STATEMENT.

" The first thing that led us to suspect Miss Greene of taking things was that one of the help missed a pair of drawers. In two weeks they came into the wash with Miss G.'s clothes, her name marked on them with blue ink. The Monday before she left she brought down a fortnight's wash (having been absent part of the week before), in which was a chemise belonging to Miss Sherburn, another to Miss Harriman, a pair of drawers to Miss Belcher, and a handkerchief to Miss Fuller; we found in her drawers a chemise belonging to Miss Case, another to one of her classmates, Miss Fuller, which she admitted she knew whose it was. I asked her why she had not returned it. She said, she supposed she should, if she had known this would have come up. There was also found a towel belonging to Miss Robinson, and another unmarked, which she said did not belong to her; two collars of Miss Case's, one of which she said at first was her own, but afterwards owned it was not; a handkerchief of Miss Straw's; a pair of under-sleeves of Miss Hunton's."

"The above-named articles — some of them were marked, but mostly unmarked — were identified and claimed by the owners herein named.

"MRS. DAGGETT, Matron."

Before I proceed to make any comment on this statement of Mrs. Daggett, I will give

THE STATEMENT OF MRS. L. M. GREENE.

"I, Louisa M. Greene, mother of M. L. Greene, hereby testify and assert, that on the thirteenth day of March, 1866, my daughters, Louise and Estelle, picked up all their articles of clothing, at the Packard house on Kent's Hill, — Estelle coming home with her father and Louise going to the college building to board. From the articles of wearing apparel, which she carried to the college at that time, and those which I carried to her on the 27th of March, and on the 11th and 14th of May, there were lost and missing (not including the towels handed to me by Mrs. Daggett, May 30th, and the articles obtained by Miss Reed in October afterwards, nor those found on the remains of Louise), which did not come home with her things after she had gone, the following articles, namely : —

5 *pairs of cotton drawers, 4 pairs of them good and nearly new;*

7 *chemises, some of them bleached, some unbleached. One of the bleached was ruffled, two were trimmed with tape trimming, one a plain yoke;*

5 *pairs of under-sleeves, one pair of them ribbed;*

2 *long linen towels with a blotted mark ('L. M. Willard') my maiden name, on them;*

1 long night-dress marked ;

1 *nice new handkerchief, plainly marked with her name, and cost* $1.00 ;

8 napkins, two of them marked, — 6 of them new ones, not cut,—put in the bottom of her trunk by me May 14th, 1866 ;

1 pair cloth boots ;

1 *tucked linen collar, which I carried her from home, May 11th, 1866* ;

3 *new collars, late style; bought them myself in May; have the impress on they were " tucked "* ;

1 box of paper collars ; bought them myself May 14th, 1866 ;

1 pair of new cotton hose, bought May 14th, and several pairs which had been worn some ;

6 skeins of black sewing-silk, which I sent her four days before she left ;

7 sticks of embroidering braid Mrs. Kent had her charged with when she left, cost $1.26 ;

All her belts, buckles, bosom-pins and cuffs, — I know she had several of each, — together with many trinkets and little fancy articles. In addition to these there were missing several valuable school-books, and four large sheets music copy paper ;

1 stone flower pot.

In all 60 articles or more lost or missing at this term only.

"LOUISA M. GREENE."

" *Oxford, ss., Aug. 24th*, 1867.

" Personally appeared Louisa M. Greene, and made oath that the above statement by her subscribed is true according to her best knowledge and belief, before me.

"ROSCOE H. THOMPSON, Justice of the Peace."

In 1864 Louise lost at the Hill two books, — one was " Golden Grains," the other " Ten Nights in a Bar-Room,"—written by T. S. Arthur.

I should not have named these small missing articles, had not such articles been named in their charges against Louise.

It must be apparent to every one, from the testimony of those connected with the institution, that the practice of putting unmarked clothing into the wash prevailed, and was indulged extensively, if not generally, at the time Louise was accused of taking clothing. Mrs. Daggett says : " The first thing that led us to suspect Miss Greene of taking things was that *one of the help* missed a pair of drawers. In two weeks they came into the wash with Miss Greene's clothes, with her name marked on them, with blue ink." It is evident then, that these were unmarked till L. marked them. The " help," as well as teachers and students, were allowed to put unmarked clothes into the wash, while she, as well as others had nothing whereby she could recognize her own except the "hems and stitches," or something of the kind. "Every like is not the same." The help might be mistaken in the drawers and claim L.'s as her own; or L. might make the same mistake with respect to those of the help. By means of exchanging, by mistakes or something of a less harmless name, L. had been the loser in the operation; and had all rooms been searched with the same relentless scrutiny as was hers, whose stubborn will to think for herself had doomed her to "walk on the Hill alone," no doubt the result of such exchanges would have been found in other rooms beside hers. I know not how it was managed, to get from L. her last pair of drawers; but it is plain this was done. "I came to the college," she says, in her letter to her sister, "with three or four good whole drawers, — two pairs which were new ones, — and to-day, as I ride away, I have none; they were lost in the wash, because unmarked."

This was true. No drawers were found on her remains, and none returned home with her clothing. Could the "help" who claimed those marked with blue ink tell anything about what became of L.'s drawers? Perhaps not; yet, somebody must know what became of them; and it was hard that, from the ample stock of clothing which she had, and all she had been accused of "taking," *she* could not have been allowed a pair of drawers in which to travel to her leafy couch of death. As Louise had plenty of drawers of her own, if they were not lost, would she have returned those to the wash that the help claimed, if she had intended to *steal* them? Does it not look more reasonable that she supposed she had found a pair of her own missing drawers, and took a pen and marked them, in hopes she should not lose them again?

An extract from a letter, dated April 14th, 1867, from a lady who had worked in the college building, will show how loose was the management in the laundry, and what other "help" were allowed to do. She says: —

"There used to be some grumbling among the students about their clothes getting mixed up. Never knew of the steward furnishing money or clothes for anything that was missing. As we were short for help to do our washing, the steward's wife told me to put my clothes in with students'. My clothes were not all marked. Towards the last of the term I missed one article of clothing, and could not find it anywhere; but on the table I found an article of the same kind, that looked very much like mine, only it was marked L. A. Jones, I think. At any rate it belonged to a young lady. She had left that week, and taken her clothes out of the wash. I made up my mind that she took her clothes in a hurry; and took, as she thought, her own, but by mistake took one article that belonged to me, and left hers.

I went to the steward's wife, and told her about it. She said, most likely that was the case. 'Any way,' said she, 'take what you have found, and keep it until you find your own.' I wore that one out, with the mark on it, and did not consider it stealing, either. I cannot think that it is anything very strange that she, or any other girl among so many, should sometimes get on clothes that do not belong to them."

"The Monday before she left," says Mrs. Daggett, "she brought down a fortnight's wash, in which was a chemise belonging to Miss Sherburne, another to Miss Harriman, a pair of drawers to Miss Belcher, and a handkerchief to Miss Fuller." Here were four stolen or "taken" articles, it seems, returned fearlessly to the wash, openly, with her own hand, without covert or concealment, to be washed, and, if unmarked, to be put upon the common pile ; if marked, of course, to be there for the claimer, or put in the owner's box. At such evidence of larceny a jury of good or common sense would smile.. But none of these articles were distinctly marked, except the old handkerchief "with holes in it," which Mrs. D. told us about. That was marked with Miss Fuller's name. To this Louise tacked another handkerchief, and said in her list, "Two handkerchiefs marked 'Miss Fuller;'" intending the mark on one to answer for both in the description, making no attempt at concealment. Mrs. Daggett has given what she may think are facts, which will answer the purpose for which they are written, without explanations or comments. I will allow Miss Sherburne to express her own views respecting the first article named as being in the "bundle" brought to the wash.

In a letter, dated at "Phillips, Jan. 29, 1867," Miss Sherburne says : —
"*Even if Louise did take some clothes from the wash, I should think nothing at all of that; for it is no more than others have done, if they could not find their own, to take what there was left. My chemise had been marked with ink, but had nearly faded out. It was not found in Louise's room, but she brought it into the wash with the rest of her clothes. Although I was but very little acquainted with your daughter, I always thought very highly of her, and I never can think that the teachers, as well as Mrs. Daggett, did just right.*"

Neither the chemise "belonging" to Miss Harriman, nor the drawers claimed by Miss Belcher, were marked. Miss Harriman writes, under date of "Feb. 1, 1867," and says: "The chemise that I lost was a new unbleached one, — not large, but rather small; had been missing some two or three weeks. I first saw it afterwards on the ironing-room table," etc. "The article was not marked, but it was made unlike any other that I saw at the school." She further says : "There were frequent complaints that articles were lost in the wash. In regard to losing other things, I lost a new nice chemise in the fall term." Who had "taken" this? Not Louise, surely; for she was no longer there, to be urged "to account for all the little things missing." Miss Belcher, in a letter dated "Feb. 28, 1867,". says: "The facts about the articles found in Miss Chapman's and your daughter's room I am unable to give, except as I heard them from the other teachers; as I did not myself enter the room, or look at any of the things. It will therefore be much better for you to ask Miss Case, Mrs. Daggett, or Miss Robinson." (An oasis in the desert.) The reader will notice that while others are continually using the term "her room, her room," Miss Belcher recognizes the fact that she had a room-mate; and that she did not enter that room to search, implicate, and claim unmarked articles. She continues: "About my things I will tell you in as few words as possible. I had missed several articles of clothing; and on Monday morning of that unhappy week, went to Mrs. Daggett, and told her I could not put my clothes in the wash again, until I could be sure of having them all returned to me. She asked me what I had lost. I told her, among other things, was a pair of new drawers, which I had put into the wash two weeks before. I knew them by certain marks which I described to her." What these "certain marks" were she does not say; perhaps peculiar stitches or hems, or something of the kind. She does not say they were marked with her name. It will be seen that they had been missing two weeks; and if they were Miss B.'s, Louise had worn them a week, and returned them into the wash. But Miss Belcher had "missed several articles." Who had taken them? They do not say they found them in the room, or pretend that L. returned to the wash any other article belonging to Miss Belcher. "She (Mrs. Daggett) next morning, I think (Tuesday), brought them to me, and asked me if those were the ones. I at once replied that they were. In the course of the forenoon I was told it was suspected that one of the girls had been taking what did not belong to her; and, later, that it was your daughter. I was very much surprised and shocked, and told the teacher who gave me the information that I would rather give her all my under-clothes than have it made public." It will here be seen that this exchange of clothing was represented to Miss B. as stealing,—a great crime. "It would be such a blow. I admired her always for her talents, which were of the highest order; and felt sure that there was something more to be explained. I know that words are powerless to comfort you; but if an assurance of my heart-felt sorrow and pity for you, when I heard of the death of one of the most talented girls I ever knew, can be of any comfort, you have this assurance." In my judgment, had the same spirit and consideration that breathes through this whole letter, from which I have made the foregoing extracts, been manifested by all concerned in this heart-rending affair, we might have been still blest with the society of our darling child, and saved the painful duty of this defence. Having shown that this article, returned to the wash in the bundle of which Mrs. Daggett speaks, was unmarked, and such as students and help had been allowed to take and wear when their own were gone, Mrs. Daggett continues: "We found in her drawer a chemise belonging to Miss Case, and another to one of her class-mates, Miss Fuller." The most I can say, in regard to the chemise claimed by Miss Case is, that L. had one just like that, which did not come home with her clothing; and the collars which she claimed and took from Louise, I believe were the same ones that Mrs. Greene carried to her, May 11, 1866. Mrs. D. told us that L. said so at first, but afterwards said they were not the ones. We shall never know in full what she did tell them about the clothing. It has been told me that they said L. at first told them that she took the articles of clothing because she was obliged to; that she had frequently lost many things there, and had borne it in silence; but now, when hers were gone, she intended to make her own number good from the pile of unmarked articles, until her own were returned. This, I believe, was the case; and, further, that they followed in accusing, arguing, pursuing, until they got her so mortified and confused that she hardly knew what she did say. She saw they meant to make it look bad as they could, and that they meant to disgrace her; but as I could not trace such admission to any reliable source, I give the above as my opinion of what Louise did say to them about the clothing. If that chemise and collars were Miss Case's, then L. had certainly lost hers; and it would not be strange if L. had taken these, thinking they were her own, she having articles like them; or anything criminal, if she took them instead of her own. As to the article of Miss Fuller, Mrs. D. says: "She (L.) admitted that she knew whose it was." Mrs. D. has tried to represent this as an article known to L. as being marked; as she did to me, Nov. 8. Had it been marked, this expression would not have occurred. They would have known that she knew whose it was, without asking. It is immaterial whether she had this through mistake, or in lieu of a lost one. She and Miss Fuller were class-mates, social and friendly as sisters. She had found out, if Mrs. D.'s statement is correct, whose chemise it was. This, it seems, gave her no particular concern or anxiety. It was going back to the wash at the usual time. She was asked " why she had not returned it." That is, I suppose, why she had not forthwith returned it, when she found out whose it was. She answers (according to D.'s recollection eight months after), " she supposed she should, if she had known this would have come up." She might have said, if she had known that, contrary to the practice with others, they would have got up this fuss. Miss Fuller writes Mrs. Greene, Feb. 1, 1867, from which I make the following extract: —

"I have hesitated to open anew the terrible wound I had no power to heal; but it cannot be unpleasant for you to hear repeated how much we loved our dear lost sister, although you know it so well already. If she had been less dear to us, or if we had been less proud of her talents and acquirements, that last blow would not have fallen upon us with such crushing weight; and although it is such a bitter thing for us, yet I feel that we cannot know the depth of your anguish when all your fears proved true, and you knew that our dear Louise could never speak again to you. Oh, it did seem almost too hard, and hardest of all to believe that a word in season to the prayer of her letter to us might have saved her! But then it was too late; and when that word might have been spoken, everybody seemed powerless to act. We were paralyzed, it seems. I can explain it to myself in no other way. The garment that Mr. Greene wished me to describe to you, was a chemise with a straight yoke, trimmed with crotchet braid, and insertion of the same trimming had been put in the band after it was made and *marked*. So that when each edge had been turned in to put in the trimming, the marking was turned in with it, so that nobody but myself would have discovered it."

This chemise, of course, must have, after being washed, gone into the unmarked pile, where L. found it.

This class-mate told me that Louise was kind-hearted and strictly honest; safely kept, and properly accounted for, all the funds that came into her hands while she was treasurer of the Adelphian Society. She never knew aught against her until this affair; and that at the time these charges and reports came out against her, they looked so *large* to us all then; but now, it looks so small; it does seem hard to think she lost her life for it. The reader will see how this was *made* to *appear* at that time before the school.

This class-mate does not think that they did all that might have been done to have saved her, as this bigoted faculty do, whose duty it was to have acted promptly to have tried to save her. Blind and self-willed are they who do not try to see.

"There were also found," says Mrs. D., "a towel belonging to Miss Robinson, and another, unmarked," which Mrs. D. says, "L. said did not belong to her." One of these no one had claimed, the last we inquired about her things there. If they were not hers, then somebody had taken them. These were the numbers which we knew she had lost, although we believe that she had several others which were not returned with her things. Mrs. Daggett gave as a reason how Miss Case knew the collars she took from L. were hers was, "because none in the college but three teachers had such a new-style collar." How did they know whose parents or friends of the sixty or more females there had not sent to them, or some one of them, in the last two weeks, or twenty-four hours, such collars as L.'s mother had done nine days before? "A handkerchief of Miss Straw's; a pair of under-sleeves of Miss Hunton's." Mrs. D. does not say that this handkerchief was marked, or whether it was like the old one, full of holes, she told us about; or whether it was like the nice new one which is missing from L.'s things, I do not know.

From the pen of the claimer, I have something definite concerning these under-sleeves. From her letter to me, dated Feb. 6, 1867, I extract the following: —

"I was very much surprised, as well as grieved, when, on the day after your daughter's departure, I was in the room with Mrs. Daggett and Mary Chapman, and Mrs. D., from L.'s drawer, held up a pair of under-sleeves and said, "These I suppose belong to some of the girls." I immediately recognized them as mine. The above-mentioned articles were of my own make, and consequently the stitches were somewhat peculiar."

These were unmarked, or she would not have been under the necessity of appealing to the "peculiar stitches" in order to recognize them. It is remarkable, that, with the loose practice allowed there, for the five pairs of under-sleeves which L. had lost, she had not taken in their stead but one pair; and there is a doubt in my mind whether Miss H. was not mistaken in these, and that any of the numerous visitors to the room she had lately left could be induced to recognize, when such care was taken to *exhibit* articles, and "suppose they belonged to other girls." I have adduced before the public the statement of Mrs. Greene, respecting the lost and missing articles, to show that circumstances strongly sustain the statement which L. made in her letter, when she spoke of those unmarked articles of clothing, and said, "As I live, I had no intention of stealing them. For every article I took I had lost one in the wash, and put those on in their stead, expecting before the term was done to find my own." This assertion must stand good and true unless proved to the contrary. Mrs. Greene purchased and provided almost all L.'s clothing, and had the best possible means of knowing what she had, and the description of each article; although L. or her mother did not make all of these articles of clothing, and neither could tell about the "peculiar stitches" or hems of her garments, as L.'s whole mind and soul seemed to be absorbed in her school duties I think it is measurably pardonable in her if she was, as one student expressed it, "careless about her clothing." She was not so careful as some about small things or peculiar stitches. I appeal to mothers who have children away from home to school, to say whether they do or not know about every article their children have of clothing.

The fact that L. had articles just like the ones claimed and taken by others does not prove that these were wrongfully claimed; but it does show the probable truth of her statement, that for every article taken, she had lost one; and that others, as well as she, might make mistakes as to the identity of such under-garments. Through mistake or otherwise, she had lost numerous articles. If, through mistake, they were in the hands of other students, after the search, censure, and the representation of the "enormity of the crime," it would be no wonder or surprise, if the holders should hesitate to bring them forward, and subject themselves to a like suspicion and reproach.

From a letter, dated Jan. 6, 1867, from a student who was at the Hill at the time L. left, I take the following:—

"While at school, I did lose a number of things in the wash. I never knew what became of them. Mrs. Daggett used to tell me that probably some one else used to get them, and I could take other unmarked clothes in the place of them."

To show that not only Mrs. D. tolerated this loose practice, but that Mr. Daggett was also cognizant of and allowed it in the gentlemen's department, I will introduce the statement of Mr. Houghton.

"For the benefit of those whom it may concern, I would here state, that in the winter and spring of 1864 and 1865, I attended school at the Maine Wesleyan Seminary, Kent's Hill, Me.; that I boarded in the college building, and was personally acquainted with Miss M. Louise Greene, then a member of that school, and can testify to her good womanly conduct, and great ability as a scholar. I would further state, that while there, in the wash I lost two articles of clothing, which were marked with the initials of my name in large capitals, which I never again received. Going to the steward in regard to the matter, he told me he would watch the wash, and if possible find them for me. Making the fact known to one of my fellow-students a few days after, he told me he had taken from the table, on which our clothes were laid after being washed, an article of the same kind, if not the same that I had lost, and that I might have it if I chose. I told him it was not mine, and I would not take it. But after some hesitation I took it and went to the steward, and told him the circumstances; asked him if I should keep them until I found mine. He told me I might, and, if I did not find what I had lost, or an owner to what I had, I might keep it; which I did, and wore the same away. This is an impartial and truthful statement.

" D. F. HOUGHTON."

Louise says, " When I missed things from the wash, I took other unmarked ones from the table and used them." She does not speak, in either of her two letters, as though she had been *there* educated to consider this a crime or a heinous offence. The same is true with respect to the expressions of other students. " It is no more than others have done," says one, " if they could not find their own, to take what was left."

I would not be understood as justifying this practice. No person living has stronger reason or more bitter cause to condemn and execrate the existence of this state of things than I. When clothing of all description was allowed in the wash, promiscuously and unmarked, from the teacher (down or up, as you please) to the kitchen girls or help; when no one was responsible for unmarked articles, and when no one looked after, to see who took the clothing, or what amount any student carried away; and when exchanges of articles were winked at, or openly tolerated; it seems hard, it seems cruel to us, that our daughter, after being drawn in by the existing state of affairs, should be made the scape-goat, to bear off the sins or errors of this whole institution. " They tried," she says, " to make me account for all the little things that have been missing through the term; but I could not. I have not had them." Then there were other articles, which they did not find with her.

I will now call the attention of the reader to that act, that mysterious " crime," as she calls it, which was beyond her comprehension, and the only thing which Louise felt that she was really censurable for. I mean the taking of that five dollars, and which she, on being asked, immediately confessed and restored. It is useless for me to repeat what I think and know about this strange act, this abrupt and hasty descent from her ever high moral standing down to an act of petty larceny. Concerning the money *she* says : " Some Satan hidden in my heart said, take it, and, before I could think, I stood again in 27. When I went in to Miss Church's room, I had no such intention in my heart." This was the first and only act of the kind she had ever done. She did not need the money. She says, in answer to the question, " Had your father been close about furnishing you with funds?" " I have always had all the money I have asked for." She made no excuse or denial, as is almost universally the course of those who commit crime, from the petty thief to the highest criminal. On being accused or arrested, they deny, prevaricate, and make all sorts of excuses. Look at the tenor of her letters, and the opinions of class-mates and fellow-students; look at her daily walk, her acts or conversation from a child; does the least appearance of a wicked heart, or a perverse mind appear, that she should conceive and commit this act on the spur of the moment, unless there was some hidden cause operating on her, and beyond her control at the time, and beyond her comprehension afterwards? Those who are conversant with passing events, and with the history of the past, know there are cases where persons, seemingly harmless and sane, have been, as they have afterwards expressed it, irresistibly tempted to reek their hands in the blood of their best friends, and those they loved most dearly. Some are tempted to destroy their own lives, and, if prevented, and the nervous excitement passes off, they will relate their experiences as an awful temptation which the enlightened mind of modern days ascribes to natural cause.

One of L.'s class-mates says, in a letter dated Dec. 28, 1866: "I know, from her letter, that Louise took that money; but I believe that, for a moment, she was under an influence she could not resist; therefore not guilty of an intentional error. The cold eyes of indifferent people cannot see this. Her letter I prize highly. I believe every word of it, and have not the slightest feelings but love and kindness for her memory." It will be noticed that, at intervals, about that time, as the term neared its close, Louise complained of her head to her mother; complained of the lack of the power of thought: "Before I could think, I stood in 27." In her affidavit Chestina says, "L. said to Miss Case, 'I feel so strange. I wish I could think, but I can't.'" Again she says in her letter: "I think, maybe, I am not exactly as I used to be while I write this, for my head whirls, and I cannot seem *to think* to say what I am trying to say." It is evident that Louise was aware that there was something unnatural and mysterious in the exercise of her mind. It does appear, by her last letters, that she might be conscious at times, or have some suspicion of the true state of her case, and true condition of her mind. "If I know myself, it was not the true, real Louise Greene that did this. She was trying to live an honest, womanly life; or if she was, indeed, drifting into disgrace, she never realized it. That five dollars is a mystery to me. What possessed me to take the money I do not know; but I took it. The moment they asked me about it, I confessed it." In her class letter she says: "I do not know what tempted me. Everything that was asked me, I told the truth about, as near as I could, in my *distracted* state of mind." Mr. Orrin Daggett, the steward, writing from Kent's Hill, Jan. 29, 1867, says: " Miss M. Louise Greene confessed to me and others that she went into Miss Florence Church's room, a few days before she (Miss Greene) left the school, and took, in the absence of Miss C., a five-dollar bill from her porte-monnaie, which she restored before she left." On the 8th day of November, 1866, I was in the college office. He (Daggett) told me that some time in the day, on the 22d of May, he was called to the room where Mrs. D., Miss C., and Louise were to assist in the examination; and, after questioning her about the clothing, — especially about two handkerchiefs she had put in the wash, — (they were, I suppose, the same ones before named: the old one with holes in it, with Miss Fuller's name faintly seen on it; the other unmarked, attached to it, and put into the wash with her written list), — he questioned her about them all he desired, then asks her about the missing five dollars. He says: " The first word she spoke, she told him where it was, not denying a word. He asked her if she would get it. She said yes, and gave it to him soon after." It will now be seen that, in this matter also, her statement in her letter was perfectly true. It will also be seen that this whole affair was all the work of a few days. Mr. Daggett, in answer to my questions, said they had not the least proof, whatever, against her, — Miss Church accusing no one of taking it; but they, finding she had a slight suspicion of some one, pressed her to know who that one was. She did not want to say, as she had no proof, — mere suspicion; said it would be of no use to say; but they drew it from her; hence his questioning L. If she had been a bad or wicked girl, an intentional thief, she would have squarely denied all knowledge of the money; that would have been an end to it; and those who knew her best, would never have believed she took the same. From a letter by a schoolmate of L.'s to her sister C., dated Oct. 24, 1866, I take the following: " Poor girl! how she must have suffered! She must have been insane, or she never would have done as she did. I loved her dearly. I presume you will never attend school at Kent's Hill again, and not to blame either. I blame the teachers very much in regard to Louise going away." Miss Harriman, who has been brought before the public as one of the claimants of one of the articles which L. took in lieu of her own, while, in the charitableness of her heart, she, no doubt, would be glad to relieve all from blame, seems to be willing that censure should fall anywhere rather than on her unfortunate and fallen school-mate. In a letter, to which I have before referred, she writes: " Louise was a favorite with all. She was talented, and, as a thorough scholar, enjoyed an enviable reputation.

All were friendly to her, both teachers and students, as far as I can judge; and that fact, perhaps, more than any other, made her wretched, and overturned the balance of her active but sensitive mind. She saw her own position in a worse light than others did." Miss H. did not consider or know who impressed upon her mind the "enormity of her crime," the hopelessness of her position, and the void and darkness of her "future;" her great object to graduate successfully, the bitter disappointment of self and friends. "The faculty of the school were also deeply engaged with care of government, and the preparatory measures for the close of term, and this very unfortunate affair took them entirely by surprise, and they may very likely have misjudged as to their duty. I know that when a fate so very sad occurs, with so many varying circumstances about it, it is usual for persons, in their deep affliction, to see faults in the management of the affair; and it would be strange if some of the persons, actors in this scene, were not blameworthy. I have sometimes felt to blame her parents, even, for keeping her so long at school, and thought that her mind had been overtaxed with study, and had become weak and ill-balanced in some direction."

Writing to us from Kent's Hill, Oct. 7, 1866, Miss M. I. Reed says: "The blow was so great that it stunned her. Poor girl! She did not have control over her own mind when she left."

From one of her classmates' communications, dated Oct. 19, 1866, I extract the following: "I am very glad to say that none of the class, to my knowledge, said they would not graduate with Louise. I cannot realize that it is our own Louise, that we loved so much, that I am writing of. It is too dreadful to think of. If I had only spoken to Louise of this, that morning! but how could we? We would believe nothing of it till she was gone. When we knew its truth we believed her good and *true*, but only *suddenly tempted*. No one of the class but feels so, and would have then received her with open arms if we could only have had the opportunity." In another letter of Miss Reed of Oct. 28, 1866, speaking of conversing with people concerning the guilt of L., she says: "All the time I was trying to make people see it in the light that I saw it. I have told this story to many strangers as well as acquaintances, and think all have said she could have been restored. Her crime was not a crime in their eyes." By the closing sentence of the certificate of the leading citizens of Peru, it will be seen that their opinion coincides with that of the students at Kent's Hill, relative to what was imputed to L. as a crime. They say: "While we freely and unhesitatingly bear testimony to the virtue and good conduct of this lamented young lady, justice to her memory impels us to say, that, in our opinion, whatever unfortunate circumstance or occurrence might have operated, directly or indirectly, as the primary cause of her untimely end, it was not her *fault* or *crime*, but her misfortune." I am authorized by the friend who originated this certificate, and obtained the signatures thereto (the town-clerk of Peru), to say, that he circulated that certificate, and, with two or three exceptions, obtained, in person, the names thereto; and that the idea contained in this last sentence was the voluntary expression of nearly all, before their attention was called to that point; that special care was taken that this point should be fully understood, and that all gave it as their opinion that, mentally, through the whole affair till her death, she was not fully herself.

Dr. Torsey, in that faculty meeting, told us that L. told him that her parents were hard, proud, and unforgiving; that she cited a case as to her mother as evidence of the truth of her statement, which I know never had existence, except in her excited and bewildered brain. If she did this, we know she was mentally deranged; for no child was ever more attached to, and tender of the feelings of, her mother. She had all confidence in whatever she said. The same could be said of her mother's feelings and respect for her; and no person on earth can make us believe that she said aught against her mother, if in her right mind. She has entries in her diaries, letters, and other writings, all through those five years, speaking of and referring to her mother in the most tender, affectionate, and respectful manner. Her conversation with students, and letters to them, and at places where she has taught school, when speaking of home and friends, all tell of the unvarying confidence, regard, and affection for her mother. She devoutly loved and respected her mother. Her mother in turn had the same love and respect for her. There existed between them an unvarying confidence and attachment. We all looked up to her as one whose counsel and advice were worthy of consideration and respect. "O mother! my mother!" were almost the last words she ever wrote.

Her appearance, writings, and actions, after Torsey's talk with, and her leaving the Hill, the place and manner of her death, are all indications of the condition of her mind. Believing that a poem, written by her when her mother was sick, would better illustrate her feelings, and would interest some readers, I will give it in full.

"LINES

"WRITTEN WHEN OUR MOTHER WAS DANGEROUSLY ILL.

"Nay, Father, spare her longer yet, and let me go;
I am not needed here; and she, our darling mother,
When she is gone, who then shall guide

THE CROWN WON BUT NOT WORN.

The little feet, and teach them how too walk the path,
The long, rough way, which leadeth on
Through briars and thorns, and over giant hills, to end
In life immortal? When the wandering one,
Footsore, and weary of the world's rough strife,
The careless crowd, whose cold indifference
Or callous selfishness falls heavily upon the sinking heart,
With faltering footsteps homeward comes, — to whose breast
Save *mother's* can he turn for sympathy, and feel
Sure of a welcome?
    What can ease the aching brow,
And calm the throbbing nerves, like the soft touch
Of *mother's* gentle hand? Who, with patient, never-ceasing care,
Prepare the soothing draught, or smooth the pillow soft,
Anticipating every want, and never thinking once of self,
Do *everything* that mortal *can* to ease the tired
And peevish sufferer? A thousand tender offices
Which strangers think not of, a *mother's* heart remembers,
And her willing hands perform. The erring child
Whose feet, unhappily, have wandered from the straight
And narrow line of duty and of right, — who like a *mother*
Can touch the hidden springs of feeling, and from forbidden fields
Bring the stray lamb back to the fold again?
    Nay, death; we *cannot* spare
Our mother! Ours is a loving family, and each is dear
Unto the other's heart; in joy and care we've ever dwelt together;
But *mother's love*, and *mother's care*, is the keystone to the arch
Of our home comfort. Sister, brother, friend, we love them all,
Yet, when God calls them home, and we awake
To a full sense of all the cares and sufferings they've left
Behind, and all the peace and joy and glory of
This heavenly home, 'tis not so hard to say, 'O God,
Thy will be done!' But of our gentle mother
Our selfish heart cries out, 'We need her most;
Sure God hath *other* angels who can sing his praise
In heaven; others can be better spared to rest within the grave.
Without her watchful care, her loving kindness, and
Her charming presence, we all should be naught.
We *cannot* spare her yet.
    True, we know that He
Who died that we might live eternally, is able
To supply our wants, and grant us needful strength
In the hour of trial; but on all the earth
There's naught that's equal to a mother's love,
And we are weak and feeble; so our hearts
Shrink from the trial hour, and so our prayer is,
And shall be, 'Spare our mother!'
        "M L. G."

Who believes that a female in her right mind would wander far into the lonely forest and there, all alone, stay and starve, or, in any way, put an end to existence? But in her last days, hours, or moments (for none can tell how long she remained there before death ensued), no eye but God saw her; no human hand was present to administer comfort; no human tongue to soothe or speak words of comfort or sympathy; no heart to share with her the anguish of that awful hour. There is no human testimony to show what her condition mentally was in those last hours, or in what manner, or from what immediate cause she died. If she died by her own hands, then no further proof of her mental derangement is wanting. Several years ago, under the pressure of poor health, with the loss of friends, she showed partial insanity or aberration of mind, which, no doubt, led her mind in a mysterious direction, not comprehended by herself after the shadow had passed off. I have referred to her condition of mind, or the signs of temporary mental derangement, the probable result of severe mental labor, combined with physical and nervous debility. I have not referred to this, her mental condition of mind, to heap censure upon those who dealt with her in her trouble on the Hill, making them appear more culpable in this matter. Gladly I would have avoided this, but duty to the character of the innocent dead forbids that I should pass over it in silence. As far as the responsibility of the actors in this cruel affair is concerned, I would willingly admit that she was rationally guilty of all she had been charged with, in as aggravated a form as those who have been interested to exculpate the actors from blame, by magnifying her misdeeds, have attempted to fix it, and there leave it with the sound judgment and intelligence of every lover of justice, mercy, and forbearance, to say whether, after the proof of her good character and standing through twenty-two years, spent in virtue's path, and after a prompt confession of the wrong, and full restoration, those who had a knowledge of the state of mind to which their rigid examination and the consciousness of the act had reduced her, were not responsible and censurable for the lack of feeling and fatal indifference that were manifested.

I had almost forgotten to take notice of the charge brought against Louise of having in her possession a skeleton key. Dr. T. says: " For *three* years she had kept a skeleton key, opening all of the students' rooms." I have no knowledge that either he or any one connected with the institution ever stated that she ever used this key for any purpose whatever. Still, from this fact being made so prominent, the public might infer that she had done so; and it seems that it was so intended that the public should so understand it. Professor Robinson does not say, as T. does, " opening all the students' rooms," but " that she had in her possession, for *two* years, a false key, which would open most of the students' room in the college." Louise, in her last testimony, says: " A skeleton key, given me years ago, I had, that looked as though I might have used it wrongfully. God knows my heart, I never did."

To her sister she writes: " You know the skeleton key I have long had, — that told against me; but after all I do not think they believed I opened rooms with it, for the purpose of taking out things. I certainly never did." It appears evident that, while they were accusing her of taking everything that had been lost through the term (as she writes), they accused her of opening students' rooms with it, for the purpose of taking out things. Or what does she mean by saying, "But after all," etc.? (after they did accuse her of using it for the purpose of taking things, and tried to impress upon her mind that they believed it.) But she still thought that they did not really believe their own accusation true.

I have before me what the receiver certifies to be a true copy of a letter from Professor Robinson, of the date, and from which I have made some extracts. I will now quote further from this letter, and let the reader judge of the truth and the logic therein expressed : " With reference to the sad case of Miss Greene, and the reports circulated about Mr. Torsey, let me say, first, that Mr. T. is no more implicated in the matter than the other members of the faculty, and if there were any blame, it ought to fall equally on us all." (Well, if R. wishes to say to the public that brother-in-law Torsey's standing and influence is worth more than all the rest of this faculty, and they wish to shoulder equal shares of his load, so be it.) I can only say, it may look rather hard for Mrs. Grover, one of the faculty, who said at the close of that faculty meeting: " That was the first time that she had heard the particulars. I would have been glad to have befriended her if I had known it." Was this fair or just to Mrs. Grover, who had nothing to do in the matter, and did not a week after know the particulars? Was it fair to say that she was equally and as much to blame as Miss Case, who did all she could to accuse, convict, and impress the crime on my poor child, and left her alone the night before she left? R. further says: "But on reviewing the matter, even in the light of the sad result, I can find nothing worthy of blame. Had we known that she would have taken her own life, we might, although we had no lawful right to do so without a warrant from a justice, have put her in close confinement; but even then, if she had determined to commit suicide, she could have found some way to accomplish her purpose." Is this sound logic — rational argument — or is it sophistry? It seems to me the learned professor must have presumed much on the simple credulity of the person addressed to advance such ideas to make his case appear justifiable. It is an argument better adapted to impose on female credulity than to meet the gaze of a reasoning public. Where is the school-boy, so dull and void of the power of invention, that could not devise some means to provide for the safety of a feeble, distracted woman, only for a few hours, without resorting to a justice warrant? But even that course would have merit, rather than suffer her to stray away to wandering or to death. And who would think of quibbling on "*lawful rights*" in such an emergency? "In the light of the sad result" we are told that had they known she would have taken her own life, they could not have done differently, could not have prevented it. Is this faculty willing to proclaim *that* to the world, to the fathers and mothers of this State, to those who send their children there? Is that what you mean when, in your catalogue, you say, "Parents may feel assured that their sons and daughters will find here a safe and pleasant home"? I put this question square to you, Mr. Robinson: Were this your child, and our situations reversed, would you, sir, be satisfied, after I had known and taught your child for five years, as you have mine, to have me proclaim to you that had I known your child would have wandered far away and died, and her remains have wasted away before you had found her; and when you had gathered up her bones, and, in great sorrow and anguish, had laid them in the grave, and life had become dreary and tiresome on account of the loss of your dear one, would you be satisfied for me to proclaim: " Had I known all before, I could not have done anything differently, done anything to have prevented so awful a result"? You would then see your miserable, contemptible logic in its true light, and would be ashamed of it. Are this faculty, who publicly announce the ability and talent, the intellectual capacity, to educate and give moral tone to the character of the youth of our State, prepared to acknowledge to the public that they did not possess the power of mind, the intellectual energy, the means sufficient, to have invented, organized, and put in operation some plan to have saved my child, if they had known the sad result of their neglect?— that they could not have listened to the proposition and advice of Miss Reed and the desire of Chestina to follow her? That, in all probability, would have saved her. Professor R.'s argument is this to the parents who send their children to that school: "If they get into trouble, and are driven to despair by their own acts or ours, and we know they intend to commit suicide, we can invent no means to prevent them." The extract I have quoted was doubtless meant for the private ear, to be breathed from private to private, till the circle partook of a public nature. I place this acknowledgment before the public. If it be true, the faculty have the benefit of it; if false, I am not responsible for it.

But it shows my position well taken and sustained, that my daughter could and ought to have been saved. The idea is preposterous that she could not have been safely detained on the Hill till I could have been sent for. Or, if Mr. Harriman had been advised, or, perhaps I ought to say, permitted, to follow her at the time he said he would, I think she would have been saved. From the fact that R. says they could not have detained her without a warrant, it is evident they had withdrawn all control over her, and " practically " expelled her from the school. Only nine days before this she asked leave to go up to Chestina's room in the evening, to see her mother and do some necessary copying, and it was refused her by Miss Case, when she knew her mother was there. The poor girl came running up the next morning, before she left, to explain why she did not come up the evening before, as her mother wished. This was the last time her mother ever saw her, and that writing she wanted her to copy will remain undone forever, as it was so faded that no one could make it out but her. They then could and did control her. But nine days after Torsey makes his miserable excuse. Robinson, in that letter, continues : " She said that she could not remain on the Hill. She knew that it was impossible to keep the matter from the students. No intimation was given her that she must leave the school, that she could not graduate; but, on the contrary, Mr. Torsey expressly said to her that if she left, it would not be on account of any action of the faculty, but of her own choice."

Mr. Robinson was present in that faculty meeting and knows that Mr. T., in giving us an account of her leaving, did not state it as he has here. He heard Torsey tell us that he advised her to go home. Will he, R. or T., say, that if L. had complied with this advice, and gone home, they expected her to come back and graduate? Robinson also heard Dr. T. distinctly tell us that L. said she could not go home; that she could not meet her folks. Why was she saying this to Torsey if he had given her no intimation about leaving, and T.'s telling us, that he told L. if she did go away he would hold her diploma and at the end of a certain time she could write him, and, if she did satisfy him that she had lived a good honest life, he would send her diploma to her? He, R., knows that he has misrepresented what Torsey told us; also he has misrepresented what L. says about the clothing, in those letters R. had seen. Hear her: " If I could have had an opportunity to retrieve the past on the Hill;" which shows that she desired an opportunity that was denied her. " ' Dr. Torsey informed me this morning that I had better leave to-day, ' not expulsion,' he said ; ' we won't call it that, but I advise you to go home.'" And when Chestina asked him if she could not have stayed and graduated, hear his answer:

"Well, no; it would not have been best for her to have gone on to the stage." It was all fixed in his mind that she should not graduate; and he speaks of it as a thing that had passed; "have been," in the past tense, is his answer to her sister. He had determined the case in his mind, but smooths it down a little to C., and says, "It would not have been best;" his determination is clearly seen in this answer to Chestina. Miss Reed says Dr. T., told me that when he asked L. what she proposed to do, she replied, "I want it kept from the school; stay, and graduate." Robinson overlooks all those statements, and in the early part of this letter says, "Miss Greene acknowledged that she had taken several articles that did not belong to her; also that she had taken money." He has evidently connected the clothing and money together, so as to give the person addressed to understand, that she confessed that she had stolen several articles as well as the money. If he intended to state *facts*, why did he not say she had lost many things in the wash, and said she took those in their stead? In her letter, she says, "When I came to the college I brought many unmarked articles of clothing, some new ones, and when I missed things from the wash I took others, unmarked, from the table, and used them. But if my own had not come by the close of the term, I should have left those where I found them, in the wash." This letter R. heard read in that faculty meeting. She further says, in the letter to her sister, "For every garment I had taken, I had lost one in the wash, and put those on in their stead. I had no intention of stealing them." The reader can but see the gross injustice done her in this professor's statement. I have already sufficiently shown that, "her own choice," of which R. speaks, was similar to the choice she had years before of remaining in Dr. T.'s house, after he had said, "Miss Greene, you will please leave the house!" Prof. R. further says, "As soon as Dr. T. learned that she had gone contrary to her promise without the knowledge of her sister, he immediately sent a student with the sister to Mr. Greene to inform him of the circumstances and to urge him to meet Louise at Lewiston. He had no idea, nor any one of the faculty, that she would take her life." I have already shown, by Dr. T.'s own letter to me, that L. never made the promise here stated. How "immediately" a student with the sister was sent to me may be seen by reference to the sworn statement of that sister. Louise left in the morning stage and reached Lewiston by noon, and it was six at night before this team started to notify me, although Miss Reed and Chestina urged immediate action, and stated plainly to Torsey that it was their belief that she would destroy herself before night. A wilful misrepresentation by R. Would he have called, from ten in the morning until six at night, or from noon until six, *immediately*, if this was his child, and then sent twenty-five miles to me, which is thirty-five miles from Lewiston, making sixty to be travelled by private team before I could get to where they knew she had gone, when twenty-five miles by team would have taken them to Lewiston? A more miserable arrangement could not have been thought of. Mr. Robinson, wofully misrepresents "facts," when he says, Torsey immediately sent a student with the sister to Mr. Greene to inform him of the circumstances, and to urge him to meet Louise at Lewiston. I hold the letter (sent by Mr. Chandler the student, who came home with Chestina) in my hand. There is not a word of information contained in that letter as to where Louise had gone, or a word of advice as to what I could or had better do to try to save, or recover her; the word Lewiston is not written in that letter, neither did Mr. Chandler or Chestina bring or deliver any word from Dr. Torsey as to when or what we had better do, or that we had better do anything to try to save or recover her. The whole gist of that letter was this, — I in that long talk with L. urged her to go to Jesus, to you, and to her mother, and tell you all, and that you would forgive her; and that Chestina will make explanations and give information concerning Louise.

Had Chestina and Harriman, or some other persons been immediately sent to Lewiston, she very likely would have been found at the Elm House, and been saved. Or, had a team been sent forthwith to me, I might have arrived in the vicinity of Lewiston in season to have discovered and saved her. This matter of accusation commenced on Monday the 21st; and through to the close my daughter was in the deepest trouble and excitement; and not until Wednesday, in the middle hours of that night, was I notified. She was accused on Monday, tried on Tuesday, sentenced on Wednesday morning, and advised to leave (expelled, they so understood it) and go home; and before I was notified of any trouble, on the third day, perhaps, her troubled spirit was in eternity.

Is there any wonder that I feel aggrieved? — that tears flow thick and fast as I write? Is there not a *cause?* I have had four daughters for a longer or shorter period at that institution, at about fifteen hundred dollars' expense. Setting aside all claims, and feelings, and *rights*, even of humanity (religion should not be named here, for it would be a disgrace to speak of it in connection with this whole transaction), would not common civility, the honor and respect due from man to man, lead me to expect, had it been my dog, instead of my child, that I should be notified before he was unceremoniously kicked from that institution?

I placed her there under their promise that she should there find a "safe and pleasant home." I had a right to expect that those under whose control I had placed er, would be her guardians, protectors, and friends; and although "of age," that their protecting care would not be withdrawn until they had returned her, or notified me, and I had time to have reached her. I was responsible, and they looked to me for her expenses. Whatever might have been her crime, their responsibility and obligations would have been increased. She should have had time to have consulted her friends, and a full investigation had, before any intimation was given her as to what the result would be about graduating. They were bound by every consideration to extend to her paternal care and protection.

Where, among my readers, is the parent or guardian, whose ward or offspring should leave his premises, as my daughter left Kent's Hill, self-disrobed of everything of seeming value in life, — self-disrobed, as it were, for the shrine of death, — who would wait in idle unconcern and indifference for eight long hours before moving in any direction for the safety of the wanderer, and then move in such direction that sixty miles should lie between the loved one in peril and him who might seek to be the preserver? What parent would not have immediately followed in the shortest direction, to save from so terrible a fate, if possible? Would doubts of any parent, in such a case, influence indecision and delay? Should a child of any parent fall into the hands of a stranger for only a few days, in such a case, and he should not look after her safety, should you not consider him recreant to duty, and false to the principles of humanity? Can you think of any sect of people anywhere, civil or otherwise, where she would have fared any worse than she did at this religious institution?

It does seem remarkable and strange, while students were so forcibly impressed with the idea that L. would destroy herself, that Dr. T., or as R. says, any of the faculty, should have no such idea! Appearances were convincing to students, and their logic was correct. A portion of the faculty, with the best of opportunities of judging and forming a correct opinion, discovered nothing convincing, to excite suspicion; no idea, no fears of such a result. Before Prof. R. closes this letter, he says: "I know a great many false reports have been circulated about Dr. Torsey, but those who know Dr. T. will not believe them. I am glad that you still feel an interest in the reputation of the school, and of your old teachers, and that you wish to correct, as far as you may, these false reports."

Then this is the object of your long string of statements, Mr. R., that you fear for the reputation of the school, and Dr. Torsey's, that you put forth such wretched *misrepresentations* and call them *facts!*

How many important facts have you suppressed to damage my daughter's side of the case, and to clear the faculty? He says, "Miss Greene acknowledged that she had taken several articles that did not belong to her." But he does not give her the benefit of the simple explanation, that they were taken from the wash, or that she had lost four times as many articles. Others quote from her letters to show her guilt and crime, without a word of explanation. Is this fair or just? They adopt these quotations as truth, to throw the blame all on her, and to exonerate the faculty, without giving her the benefit of her own dying explanation. And here I would say, that both *law* and *sound reason* will forbid those who quote from her confession, in those letters, and adopt as true such portions as they choose; they are estopped in denying the truth of the whole. Prof. R. closes his epistle to his correspondent as follows, —

"God, who knows our hearts, knows that we have no feeling of harshness or severity towards Louise, nor of *vindictiveness* towards her friends. Our feelings were all pity and sympathy for her, and only pity for her unhappy friends." Thus attempting to give force to those remarkable "*facts*" which he had stated, by clinching them in the name of religion and Almighty God.

The reader will judge of the pity and sympathy that were manifested, from the stern facts which transpired at the time. Was there much pity and sympathy manifested, after every means, seemingly, had been employed, to bring her mind to believe she had sunk to rise no more, — that she had committed a heinous offence, that could never be forgiven by God or man, — to leave her in her own room alone, through that solitary night, to pace it in lonely wakefulness till morn, forsaken, as it seemed to her, by God and *man?*

"I tried to read my Bible last night," she says, "but I couldn't. I don't believe I shall ever pray again, except to say 'Father, forgive me;' and he will not hear. The Saviour is an iron door, I think, to me; shut, bolted."

Was it strange, in her bewildered and excited state of mind, if the logical powers of those in whose opinion she had been taught to confide had been exerted to impress on her mind the enormity of her crime, that this idea should take possession of her deranged mind? While she was thus walking her room alone, could those who, the day previous, had investigated, even to the linen on her body, to find the mark, and must know the deplorable state of her mind, rest in quiet slumber, and call this sympathy and pity? Who would crave such?

"Mr. Schwaglerl said to me this morning, 'Remember your Saviour.' I have been saying it over all the way here."

The only thing, it would appear, that had been said to her, which she could " say over," remember, or repeat. It was the only thing said to her for which she *desired* to return thanks.

"I thank him for that, always. Mary Chapman, you tell him so."

With all the pity and sympathy in their hearts, of which R. speaks, were there no kind words spoken by any of the faculty to soothe and comfort her, which in her mind she could say over in her desponding moments while on this solitary travel? No kind words spoken by them in their pity and deep sympathy worthy of her last thanks? Would she have forgotten them, and remembered Mr. Schwaglerl's only, had such been spoken?

Yet she complains not, nor speaks ill of any one. She was not in the habit of so doing. Her disposition was not to rail, or find fault with others. As a school-mate of hers writes, under date of Oct. 25, 1866: —

"It seems as though words were a mockery, when speaking of our sister Louise, and the wrongs done her. I never heard her speak ill of any one but Dr. Torsey. Oh! if she could have known what a wrong he would have done her, how much more she would have disliked him!"

It is possible Prof. R. might be right, asserting as a "fact," that he had no feelings but pity and sympathy for Louise; but how he could assert understandingly, and have the assurance to call his Maker to witness the truth of assertions respecting the feelings of others, is not so easy to understand. He was not present at that very "private investigation," or at that long conversation T. had with Louise the morning she left. Had he been present at those conversations and investigations, he could better have judged their feelings and treatment of her; but then it would have been presumptive to have asserted positively, with an appeal to God for the truth of his statement.

If their feelings were all pity and sympathy, then I must say, they had a strange way of showing it. I cannot believe his assertions, neither do others. A correspondent, writing from Kent's Hill under date of Dec. 31, 1866, among other things, writes as follows: —

"I have buried those that were dear as life, and it was hard to give them up, and consign them to the silent grave; but God took them in his own time, and I have no right to murmur. When we have affliction come upon us in an aggravated form, it is hard to reconcile our minds to it. How could I? 'Woe unto them by whom offence cometh.'

"My mind is the same now that it ever has been, with regard to your daughter; that is, she was shamefully wronged by those that should have been her friends in the hour of trial. If her friends had all been as true as Miss Reed, there would have been no trouble, I think. Although I was not personally acquainted with your daughter, I have ever heard her spoken of in the highest terms, until she left the Hill."

This was not an isolated expression of opinion among those who were conversant with affairs on Kent's Hill at that time. In a letter, dated Jan. 6, 1867, I find the following expressions: —

"I don't care what Mrs. Daggett says, I know the students all loved Louise, — all that knew her; and the old students that were at the Hill last Exhibition, did not enjoy themselves one bit, they felt so bad about her; and many of them only stayed one night at the Hill. I don't wonder that you think so hard of the teachers. If it were me, I should be more bitter than you are. I am not afraid to tell any one that I blame them; not even Dr. Torsey himself."

In no communication that I had seen, either from students, or from any person living on Kent's Hill, or from any of the faculty, directed to me or to any other person during those five years, was one word written against the character of Louise previous to that sad affair. On the 20th of March, 1867, Torsey wrote to another person, in which he puts in an insinuating slur about a report he says was in circulation about L. I, or the person written to, have not, from that day to the present, heard a sound from any other person about the report he named. This is the only solitary case where a word *even* of insinuation against her character, up to the present time, have I seen written; or heard a word spoken against her character previous to the last fatal affair. This foreshadows what Torsey may yet attempt to do.

As fear or favoritism is I think the ruling passion on Kent's Hill, it will be readily perceived, that while surrounded by this influence, and the subordinate position, and the danger of giving offence, many would naturally hesitate, before voluntarily giving expression to their real convictions. Yet, I find all the expressions of opinions that have been ventured, as far as I know, coming from students, with one or two exceptions, blame Torsey and the others that had to do with her in that affair; meaning also to except that committee of students' actions, and those who really did indorse them.

And here I ought to say, that a large portion of the old students who knew L. so well, had left the school, and many new and young students had taken their places. And, also, I do know, that some of the old students did not attend chapel exercises on May 7th, the night that those resolutions were adopted.

This may have been one of the causes of Dr. Torsey's "pimps and spies" attack on Miss Reed, and his close watch after, and to see the communications she received from me.

In answer to a request of the town clerk of Peru, for a statement of Louise's character, as she understood it to be at that school, previous to this last affair, for publication, one of her class writes as follows, under te of Dec. 21, 1866 : " —

" I would gladly comply with your request, if it would in *any way* benefit our departed class-mate ; and I am willing to do *much* to alleviate the sorrows which oppress her bereaved parents. Such a statement as you propose *may* accomplish the latter, and it may seem a trivial act comparatively in behalf of her I loved; yet I must refuse, at the risk of being misunderstood by so doing. Such a publicity cannot benefit poor Louise, and *may* reflect upon the officers and institution at Kent's Hill."

She was not requested to give a statement of good or bad character, but such as she understood it to be. If that statement had been bad, it would not have alleviated our sorrow, and would it have reflected upon the officers and institution? We have here by inference that it must have been a statement of her good character. I would remind this class-mate of that sentiment, "Truth crushed to earth will rise again."

I will now notice how that "pity for her unhappy friends," of which Robinson writes, was manifested. While I was searching for our lost child, overwhelmed with trouble, anguish of mind, and awful suspense, absent from my family most of the time, which on account of this terrible shock were in a condition to need all my care and attention, all sorts of reports were in circulation, and continually reaching my ears, of what Louise had done, and what had been said about her at Kent's Hill, — all tending to disturb, distress, and harass my almost distracted mind, and that of my family. To know the truth of one of the reports in circulation, I wrote to Dr. T. as follows : —

"*Peru, June* 27, 1866.

" Dr. Torsey : Sir, — Nearly five weeks spent in the search, — I can find no reliable trace of her, our dear lost one. Is it a fact that Louise has all the way along, ever since she first came to your school, been thieving? Tell us all, I beg of you. It comes to us that you have said so.

"Yours respectfully,   Jonas Greene."

The reader will notice that I did not ask him what he had said, but begged of him to tell us all the facts relative to her thieving. To this letter I received the following answer : —

7

"*Kent's Hill*, June 30, 1866.

Mr. Greene, — I have not made the statement you name in your letter. Have you directly or indirectly said we expelled Louise from the school? Have you in substance said, our reason for expelling her was because she would not join the church? Have you said that her taking clothing, etc., was named to the school at prayers, or at the table? Have you ever denied she took money? Have you said she took but two or three articles of clothing in exchange for what she had lost? Have you said that any of the officers of the institution have sanctioned the exchange of clothing in the way you say Louise exchanged? Such reports as these may *oblige* us to state the facts publicly." [After stating the charges against L., which appear in an extract in the first part of this work, he closes as follows:] "She was not expelled, and no intimation was given to her that she would be. The matter was never alluded to before the school.

"Yours truly,
"H. P. Torsey."

He does not answer my one simple question, but catechises me in a string of half a dozen interrogatories, clinching them with a threat to make the matter public, in order (as I believed) to frighten me into silence. He did not answer my question (as it is seen by the mass of evidence herein presented), as he should and could have done in four words, '*No, she has not.*' But here can plainly be *seen*, this sly, low, cunning, wiry, wicked man, in his true light. He takes this opportunity (in my greatest trial, weighed down almost in despair, tired and weak in body and mind) to make the most he could of this circumstance, and leaves it open for me to infer that he could say so (that she had been thieving all along), if I provoked him. I commenced to answer this very pitying and sympathizing letter; but some new information caused me to leave home again, in a hurry, to continue my search, and I did not finish it. When I returned home, I found another of those missives, directed by that feeling of pity of which Prof. R. speaks, which reads as follows: —

"*Kent's Hill*, July 11, 1866.

"Mr. Greene, — Is it true that you told Mr. White, of Buckfield, that Louise simply exchanged clothes, — her case brought before the school, — she charged with falsehood, and expelled at once? And what story did your wife report at Mr. Perly's, at Livermore? If you are circulating such reports, it seems to me unfortunate to Louise and yourself. You know she stole money, and can find no one that will tell you I ever brought the matter before the school. If you do not think any of these things against L. are true, you can have all these and other matters pertaining to her character, or your relation to this affair, legally established or refuted, by bringing a case of libel or slander, followed on our part by a prosecution for malicious prosecution and for slander.

"Yours,
"H. P. TORSEY."

In former times, when my purse was open to the claims of that institution, letters came from him to my address with some title, as is the custom of the day; but these came simply to "Jonas Greene,"— pity having disrobed my name of even Mr. prefixed. At that time the accusations against L. had been made as public as was the fact of her disappearance; and they were exaggerated as they floated from ear to ear, or were magnified when first set afloat. To these were added in their circulation base scandal, vile insinuations, at which the very dust of my injured daughter might blush. This being the case, I could not conceive how the circulation of such reports as T. named, whether true or false, could be any more unfortunate to L., unless it was meant that I should understand that there was something worse to bring to the public ear than had been put in circulation by private tongues. This hinting at, advising, or threatening a double lawsuit, this talk about libels, prosecutions, and slander, while with aching head and heart I was hunting day and night for our loved child, whose remains lay decomposing in the lonely forest, did not sound to me at that time much like the sympathizing voice of a pitying friend. Such friends you, kind reader, under like circumstances, would desire to be few and far between. The second and last letter which I have written to Dr. T., was in answer to the two which I have noticed, and is as follows: —

"*Peru, August* 29, 1866.

"DR. TORSEY: Sir, — Your refusal to answer the one question I asked you, in my letter of June 27, puts me under no obligation to answer your various questions of the 30th of June. My whole time having been spent, from May 24 to the 1st of July, in search of our dear lost one, I had no time to properly answer it until I received yours of July 11. The spirit and address of those letters were such, coming to me in such an awful state of mind, and under such terrible trouble, — the terribly distressed state of my whole family, the pressing care of my family after being absent from them so long, — under such circumstances, I did not feel disposed to answer them then.

"I have not said you expelled her because she would not join the church; never have said that the taking of clothing was named to her at prayers or at the 'table; have never denied her taking money; have never named the number of articles she took in exchange. I know nothing about the officers of your school sanctioning the exchange of clothing, except what a student told me. I have said what he told me. I never told Mr. White, of Buckfield, what you asked me if I did. You say she was not expelled. What did you say to her about leaving the school? Did you, or did you not tell Louise that she had better leave that day (May 23), and go home? An answer is requested.

"Yours respectfully,
"JONAS GREENE."

He (T.) has never answered this question; its truth he wishes to evade. I have taken copies of every letter I have written him, at the time, and since he turned her out of his house, and the reader can see how much cause, if any, I have given him, that he should write me those insulting letters, before named. They can judge as well as I, for I have laid before the public all and every word I have written him; and you can but bear witness that I have held my temper well, and written him respectfully. I desired to give him no cause, but to see how far he, with his malignity, would go. I received but one more letter from him, which was dated October 29, 1866, after her remains were found, — his logic false, that she was going into the factory, running away, or going to other bad places, as has been insinuated.

"MR. GREENE, — You and I are to face each other at the judgment-day. It will then be known who *is* responsible for Louise's awful death. It will then be known *who* is wrong and *who has been wronged*. In view of that day I again say, I in *no* way referred to the matter before the school in her presence or *absence*, nor named it to individuals. When Miss Case named the matter to me, I requested her to say nothing of it. I did *not* tell L. she could not graduate. I told her the trustees voted the diplomas, and I would be her friend in the matter. I spoke only of any time of her leaving when *she* had decided to go home *that day*. She was not willing to see *you here*. I had no unkind *feeling towards her;* nothing *but deep* sorrow at what had occurred.

"Yours,
"H. P. TORSEY."

Whether this was intended as his letter of condolence to me, I am unable to say; but it does look more like an attempt to acquit himself from blame, by base *insinuations*, and his *denials* of what all the *circumstances* and *surroundings*, with her written declarations, and other evidences, sustain, than sympathy for the sad and final result. This is his third written denial to me that he had not referred to the matter before the school, when I had never accused him of so doing, and had written him so. "I did not tell L. she could not graduate." What difference did it make to her whether he told her she was expelled, or that he said, "We won't call it expulsion; but I advise you to go home to-day." (A slimsy dodge, indeed.) He here says, "I told her the trustees voted the diplomas, and I would be her friend." As much as to say, I will be her friend to try to obtain from the trustees her diploma. When he distinctly told us, in that faculty meeting, that "if she did go away, I would hold her diploma. She could write me in six months, or a year, and if she did then satisfy me of her good behavior, or good conduct, he would send her diploma to her." There was no trouble then but what he could do as he pleased with her diploma (which she knew was about made out before she left), which no doubt he holds to this day. Again he says, "I spoke only of any time of her leaving when she had decided to go home that day." If this be true, why did he tell and repeat over again and again in that faculty meeting, that she, all in tears, *told him* (at his request or advice to go home) she could *not* go *home*. She could *not meet her parents*. As to his assertion that he had no unkind feelings towards her, nothing but deep sorrow, with all the evidence of his prejudice and conduct towards her for the last two years which she remained on the Hill, herein produced, I will leave an intelligent reading public to judge of the correctness of his assertions.

HER PIETY DOUBTED.

Dr. T. says that he had lost confidence in her religious character. If that is so, I can only say that it appears by the memorandum in her diary, her letters, and what she had told us, that she long since came to a worse conclusion as to his Christian character. She had long believed him deceptive and void of true Christian piety. His opinion might be founded on prejudice, as I have already shown that it existed.

A school-mate writes to Louise, April 29, 1865, and among other things says: "The gist of the whole matter is, Dr. Torsey has found out that you are shrewder than he; therefore you can expect but little forbearance from the teachers. The whole course of reasoning, when sifted down, resolves itself into that." In speaking of the matter of religion, another schoolmate writes: "I am glad you spoke freely with the venerable doctor. How much did he hear from others? I read that part of your letter to my dear friend, Miss G. She said she thought interfering with religion most too much for him to attend to, especially on hearing her say she has taught fifteen years, and had never heard of such school discipline." None but God knows the depth of piety in the heart of Dr. T. or my daughter. We can judge of the tree only by its fruit. The first evidence we have of her religious tendency, and Christian faith and hope, is a letter dated at Kent's Hill, May 4, 1862, addressed to her "dear mother," in which she speaks of the death of her teacher, Prof. Scott, in the most touching terms, as an excellent man, a kind teacher, who had suddenly passed away. She there unfolds to her mother, that she had for a long time tried to love and serve God; had not had strength to publicly proclaim the fact; but that she then had resolved to bear the cross. "I love God" (she says), "and know that he will give me strength to do my duty, and lean on Jesus, and pray God to deliver me from temptation, and keep me from evil; and may I spend my days in his service."

She afterward wrote her mother, asking her if she should join the class or speak in meeting, when she did not feel it a duty to do so. She said they tell her there that she could not be a Christian without she did so. Her mother wrote her that she alone was accountable to her God for the performance of such duties; and it was not for her, or any of the teachers, or Dr. Torsey, to dictate to her what these duties should be. The hard things which I have heretofore stated that some of the faculty had said to her, had so wounded her feelings that she could not consistently go to social meetings and take a part in them on the Hill. She said she had no freedom in them. At the first of the term, in December, 1865, her sister Estelle went to the school, and was boarding with Louise in the Packard house. This was soon after Estelle had made a profession of religion. As Estelle was getting ready to go to the first class-meeting for the term, she said to Louise, "Are you not going to meeting?" L. said, "I cannot go," and began to weep. She afterward told Estelle that the reason was that it was said by some of the faculty, she went to gain the regards of a certain gentleman; and that one of them had said it made him mad to see her at class-meeting after she had said "darned fool;" or at least she had been told that it was so. But still they were finding fault with her because she did not go to their meetings more. On the 23d of December, 1866, Louise and Estelle were sent for in the night to come home, which they did on the 25th, in season to witness the death of their youngest brother, seven years old. He was buried on the 27th; he died the 25th. In Louise's memoranda I find, December 25, 1865, this entry: "At a quarter past three, A. M., God let him go, our dear mother's Christmas gift, to God. Mother has quite given up, and seems unlike her own brave self. 27th. We all went to prayer-meeting, and God there took away my cross. I had always dreaded speaking in meeting. To-night, for the first time, I could not wait till it came my turn, till the minister was done. A new and joyful state of mind for me, truly! I stayed with Abby to-night, and for the first time found strength to pray aloud. How I dread going back to K. H., where now I cannot consistently go to social meetings and be an actor therein! I'm resolved to be an active Christian, out of meetings, with God's help." Why she speaks of God's letting him go, was because he in his last hours suffered greatly, breathing so he could be heard all over the house, and it was relief to us when his suffering was over. That this record is true, as far as Mrs. Newton is mentioned, I will let her testify.

"*Peru*, March 15, 1867.

"I, Abby G. Newton, wife of W. S. Newton, who live close to Mr. Greene, hereby certify that Miss M. Louise Greene stopped over night with me on the 27th or 28th of December, 1865, my husband being absent. She (L.) read in the Bible, and then prayed with me, and talked about a Christian life and the future state. Her talk was of a high order, coming from a gifted mind. It made a lasting impression on my mind. This was the last time that I saw her.

"Abby G. Newton."

December 28th she has this entry: "To-morrow we go; and then from morning till night mother will be all alone." I did go with her and Estelle, on the 29th, to the Hill, and poor Louise never returned. December 30th she has the record: "Father went home this morning, but not until he knelt down and prayed with me. The first prayer I ever heard him make; the first prayer he ever heard me make. We shall not forget them." This was all true; she prayed when I was done. "December 31, Sunday. Sermon, P. M., on recognition of friends in heaven, Matthew viii. 11, by Rev. John Caldwell, of Hallowell. Every word seemed meant for me. I could not refrain from tears. It stirred up nobler thoughts than I believed myself capable of thinking."

As all her writings of which we have any knowledge or means of knowing the facts therein written we know to be true, we have good reason to believe that all her other writings are equally true. As there seems to be a disposition manifested by her accusers at the Hill to attack her at every point, I have felt compelled to make it clear and plain that her memoranda and her other writings were reliable, and that she possessed the power of memory to quote verbatim the language which she had recently heard. In a lengthy letter of several sheets, written to her mother, we have the substance of that beautiful sermon, referred to before, of December 31. In quotations written out from memory, in her copy-book, she has almost entire lectures written from memory after she had returned from the place where they were delivered. In her other writings she often speaks of things as they transpired at Kent's Hill. She there tells of a long interview and lecture from Dr. T., which I have laid before my readers, and we believe every word of it correct and true in substance. I believe the same of her last letter. I have before alluded to Dr. T.'s telling us that L. said we were hard, proud, and unforgiving, especially her mother. I have no means of knowing the truth of this statement of the doctor, but must repeat, if true, it shows conclusively to me that her mind was in a bewildered state. No mother and daughter ever exercised towards each other more intimate confidence, love, and kindness than did they. I will give a letter, written by L. to her mother, to show, in a measure, her feelings. It was written at Kent's Hill, December 23, 1865, the evening before the messenger arrived to bring them home on account of the dangerous illness of her brother: —

"*Saturday Evening, December* 23.

"My darling Mother, — We had a letter from Chestina to-night, and after reading it I felt like writing to you. No mail can go till Monday. How I wish it could reach you to-night! Estelle has just gone to class-meeting. I warrant you she won't forget the home friends. Wilma wrote us she had become interested in religious matters. She is young, but I think will be decided. Don't it rejoice your heart, mother, to see them all coming into the fold, to the tender arms of the Good Shepherd? If ours could become a united religious family I think it would help, in a measure, to do away with the difference so common among lots of children of nearly the same age. When I spoke just now about the children's coming into the fold, I could not help thinking that maybe the Good Shepherd would be wanting some of them up yonder, — would be taking them indeed and in truth to his fold. Ours has been an unbroken family, but it cannot be always so; and if one must go, who better than the little one, the sinless, for 'Of such is the kingdom of Heaven'? Dear mother; you would not be unreconciled, unconsolable, if what we all fear shall happen? I have thought much about George Henry lately, and it seems to me he is going. I seem to have him constantly in mind, and more especially, within a few days, him and *you*. I don't know but I worry about you more than I do about him. Are not you tiring yourself all out, mother, and preparing another sick-bed? Are there none to whose care you can trust him, at least, a part of the time? Remember, mother, you cannot endure all that you once could. You must see yourself that you are by no means as strong now as you used to be. *Your* day of hard work is done; you have had more than your share of it always. Now let the rest take their turn. Of course you cannot lay aside anxiety, but the work, the actual care of the child, should fall partly into other hands. Are not the people ready and willing? Won't they feel — or, rather, how will they feel if you won't let any of them do anything? Couldn't you feel willing, any way, to let at least Sabrina stay with George H. some, nights? I don't suppose you realize how much you are doing, and how tired you are getting; but by and by, when the uncertainty is ended, if not before, *you* will be the one needing care and medicine, if you are not careful of yourself. *Do* try and not do too much, mother; and don't wear yourself out with worrying, for is he not in God's hands, to do with him as he sees best? It seems to me that I can have perfect faith in the result; that somehow or other it will be for the best. Now, mother, won't you try and 'be a good girl,' as you used to write it in your letters to me? I hardly expect you to answer this, but wish you could write. We are getting on quite well, and mean to make things last, so we need not trouble you for things during this sickness. So don't once think of that. I wish I could do something for you, but it seems now that the most we can do is to keep from making trouble. Now, goodby, dear, with much love from your affectionate daughter,

"L. M. GREENE."

After she had returned to college, subsequent to the death and burial of her little brother, she wrote her mother as follows: —

"*Kent's Hill, Me., January* 8, 1867.

"MY DEAR MOTHER, — I ought to have written home before this, and should if I had consulted my own inclinations; but work seemed to call in another direction. Though it is only a week, we are quite well settled back into our old way of life. Only study seems tenfold harder than it ever was before. I find myself away off, thinking such strange, wild thoughts as only those who have just buried their dead *can* think. It seems providential that for this and the past term my studies are so few; for with the full number I could never in the world have got through. This past experience has made me fearful. I cannot help wondering what will come next. But I try to 'let the future take care of itself.' O mother, you should have been here last Sunday, and heard a real live sermon, that would have filled your whole soul with faith, and *made you* believe, what every one wants to believe, in the recognition of friends in heaven. Wasn't it strange that a sermon, especially suited to us, should have been preached to us just after our return? I wish father had stayed over Sunday just to hear that. It was worth coming here on purpose for. The text was from Matthew viii. 11. [She goes on to give the substance of that sermon from recollection; but it is too lengthy for my limits. She closes with these words:] "I can't help thinking of two weeks ago to-night, and it unfits me for work. Good-by, mother. Write all who can to Louise."

I have copied these letters to show the religious tendency of her mind, and the love, confidence, and affection manifested towards her mother, and her tender solicitude for her welfare. The feelings here exhibited were ever reciprocal between her and her mother; and it is with me incredible that, in her right mind, she could drop so suddenly from her high moral standing, social and religious, so low as not only to commit a petty crime, but also to speak of that dear mother in terms of disrespect, to the very man in whose friendship she had no confidence, and whose threats she had so long dreaded! She told her mother, in October, 1865, that she did not believe she should ever graduate. Her mother asked her why she thought so. She said, "I can't walk straight enough to suit Dr. Torsey. He notices little things in me that he does not in other students," and mentioned several instances. "They seem to be watching me all the time, and I am afraid that Torsey's prejudice has influenced the other teachers against me."

The loss of our little son was the first inroad made by death in our family, and it was to us all, seemingly, a sad affliction, till experience taught us that burying our friends under ordinary circumstances was comparatively a pleasure. This stroke of affliction hung heavily upon the mind of Louise, producing those "strange, wild thoughts" of which she speaks. While away from home, friends, and in combination with other circumstances and matters, the presentiment that she should never graduate, operated to bring her mind into the condition and state which I have before mentioned. It was the loss of this brother, no doubt, to which she alluded, when she said to her class, "This good-by is a thousand times more bitter than was the laying away of my dead." We, the surviving friends, can take up the expression and say truly that parting with her, under the circumstances, was a thousand times more bitter than was the laying away of all our previous dead.

Suppose, kind reader (if a parent), this was your child, your daughter, your first-born, whom from infancy you had watched over; one on whom you had bestowed your tenderest care in sickness and in health; you had watched the expansion of her mind and the development of intellect; and, with much anxiety and toil, had sought to store that mind, at home and at school, with useful knowledge. As time advanced and intellect expanded, you saw evidence of brilliant talents, and an aptness to learn; you looked on her with pride and satisfaction, doted on her as an affectionate parent only can, and looked forward with hope to the pleasing prospect when that intellect, that active mind should become matured and shine forth in the full development of womanhood. In due time you send that daughter to a literary institution, under fair promises of safety, for the purpose of acquiring a literary education. Term after term passes, years roll round, and you find your daughter making all the advancement reasonably required or expected. As a scholar, her reputation rises as she advances, and not only keeps pace with her opportunities, but keeps in advance of them. As a scholar, the most envious dares not deny the meed of praise; as a teacher, you see her successful at every trial, loved by her pupils, loved and respected by her employers and those in superior standing; you hear her character spoken of in the highest terms; you hear her abilities extolled, and her disposition spoken of with admiration; you see her, after years of anxiety and toil with books and problems, grappling with all the vexation and trials that lay between her and the goal of her ambition, with a zeal and earnest resolution which deserve success; you see her diligent by day, and frequently through the lonely night till the still hours of morning, pursuing those studies, the consummation of which is to be her final triumph; you see her progressing prosperously till within twelve days of her final triumph, for which she had so long toiled and for which you had looked with anxious mind and high hopes. All at once the curtain falls, — the dark future lies before her, all her high hopes are blasted, — her character gone, — accused of crime, — a close search made, and the search pursued to her sister's room, and even to her own body; attempts are made to hold her accountable for all the petty plunder or mistakes of the whole institution, and to impress the enormity of the crime upon her already distracted mind. No friend is notified of her situation, no friendly advice or counsel called to help her in her bewilderment to explain the dark " mystery" that shrouded her mind. Some articles of common wearing apparel are found in their room, or in her possession, while four times the number of hers are gone. No explanation is seemingly heeded. She is adjudged guilty, and the verdict goes out to her companions, the school, and to the world. No friendly teachers call to comfort or advise her; no room-mate enters for the night her apartment. Alone in her sorrow she walks her room through the dark hours of night, her brain on fire, while her mental thoughts, her very soul seems oozing from her eyes in floods of tears. The morning dawns; and your sorrow-stricken child is visited by her tutor,—by him to whose safe-keeping you had consigned her. In a long conversation she is given to understand the penalty of the acts with which she is charged, and the reality of which she had long feared. As an opiate to her troubled and distracted mind, she is told and urged to go to God, and her parents, and make great and humble confession, thus making it appear as though she had committed a great crime. She is advised to go to God for that consolation, comfort, and pardon that was denied her by man. He, Torsey, has nowhere written or said, to my knowledge, that he told her he or the faculty would forgive her. She leaves the scene of this long conversation, in which she had been advised to leave that institution, divests herself of everything valuable, writes that her heart was breaking, and wanders off alone. This is known, yet no one who has the charge of your child seems to care for, or moves to look after her safety. She is seen in her soiled clothing, the same day, wandering and weeping among strangers. During the three days in which these cruel acts are transpiring, you are only twenty-five miles away, yet no means are taken to notify you that your daughter was in trouble. No notice reaches you until fourteen hours after the fatal journey is taken. You make all haste to pursue her, but it is too late. No more is seen or heard of her till nearly five months after, when her wasted form is found in a solitary forest. Kind parent, were this your daughter, could you feel to say that "in the light of the sad result you could find nothing worthy of blame?" If so, then I would say that in my opinion, if you had to take our place, suffer (only for one month) as much as I and my poor wife did, no person would ever after hear you trying to excuse Dr. Torsey and that faculty from all blame. I care not what your religious sentiments are, if it were your case,— your child,— you would see and feel that a great wrong had been done her, and that those whose duty it was to care for and protect her until you were notified and had time to reach her, had wofully neglected their plain duty. Will Torsey say they were under no obligation to notify us? Suppose she had suddenly been taken with brain fever, her reason gone,— would he have had no duty to perform? Again, if she had fallen and nearly destroyed life, would he or his friends say he had no duty to perform? Would he have abandoned her? In such cases, he would be held in *law* for damages; but when her character was at stake, which to her was dearer than life, he could see no danger, had no fears, no immediate duty to perform. You would feel that morally, if not legally, they were responsible for her death. You would care not how high or low were their standing, — they should stand or fall by the justice of their acts. There is no religion in profession. By their acts they should be judged. By the fruit the tree is known. To do *Christ*-like is Christianity. Does the reader see anything like *his* example and precepts in all their dealings with Louise? Tell me what single act of kindness have those Kent's Hill professed Christians done in pursuing to recover, or to assist us to find our child, their old student of five years. No, not one single act or one dollar can they show that they have expended in the search, or in any way to assist us in the discovery of the one for whose board, tuition, and books I had paid them so much. They never have offered to do the first thing in that direction, or, to my knowledge, have they ever asked or requested any student to assist us, except the one who came home with Chestina; while many a stranger has turned out to assist us in the search, and many were the acts of generosity and kindness done and offered me in my long, lonely, and wearisome search, which cheered and sustained me on my sad journey. They will long be remembered; while from those managers on Kent's Hill where I have paid my money, and have so sadly lost my child, I receive only insult and injustice at every turn. What is the cause of all this? What have I done to deserve such treatment?

"I have but little faith in man. God is our only refuge in this great trial. He is merciful and good. 'His mercy endureth forever.'"

On reading the following letter of L. to her mother, — which was overlooked, — I am tempted to put it in here, although out of place: —

"*Kent's Hill, Sunday, Feb. 4, 1866.*

"DEAR MOTHER, — We received your letter last night, and will to-day commence an answer, which I shall probably mail about the middle of the week. I was both sorry and glad when your letter came; glad that this revival of religion was getting deeper into the hearts of the people, and spreading from neighborhood to neighborhood. No one can help rejoicing at this; sorry that for you, mother dear, there does not come peace, — 'peace like a river.' I believe it is waiting for you, — and not on the other shore, but here, right here. For those who are gone you can but feel thankful. I shall always think of our little one as a bright spirit, waiting just beyond the river, and rejoicing when he sees us doing bravely our life-work here, and saddened (perhaps), if we grow *too* weary of the way, too impatient for the journey's end. You ask a strange question, mother, — ' What does one like me have to live for?' I should answer, ' Everything.' For your children. Do you want *them* obliged to walk the hard path *your* childhood's feet once trod? Can you think of a sadder word for them than this one, — motherless?

"For your husband. Needs he not you, temporally and spiritually, mentally and morally? For community. You have means; you have influence. Wherein they are weak, strengthen them, and, by so doing, you will gain strength yourself. Wherein they are wrong, make yourself able, by reading and thought and word, to right them.

"When they have trouble, comfort and help them, and comfort will come into your own heart. Look not mournfully back upon the past, but hopefully into the future.

"Oh, it's very easy to say these things, but *hard* to *begin* to do them! Once begun, however, they bring their own reward, like every other good thing. Won't you try, mother mine, to turn your mind away from these sad thoughts? — to come out of self? For it is your loss you mourn, *not his*, for his is gain. Not so much your *loss*, but *losses*, I should have said. I think I understand how this bereavement has brought all the others fresh to your mind, — from the mother who left you in childhood, down through the long line to your boy. They are calling you, and it seems as though you could not wait. But think who hold you here. By the memory of your own motherless girlhood, and the need you have, *even now*, of a mother, I entreat you to find room in your heart for your other children, — and a willingness to stay.

"You are anxious to go, you say; *anxious* to leave us to — what? Do you realize what? Can you imagine our home *as* a home, and you gone? Do you want your children to grow up as Aunt Martha's would have grown without your care? You are willing, ' nay, more, *anxious* for this'? Take it back, mother, unsay it; you cannot mean it, mother. You might be willing for us all to die and you be left, but must not be willing for the opposite.

"You used to be strong and brave. It is twice as heroic to be willing to live sometimes, as it would be to die as the martyrs did, — at the stake.

"Don't pray for death, — but patience, faith, and strength. May you have them always and abundantly, is the earnest wish of

"Your affectionate daughter,

"LOUISE."

The denomination in the interest in which this school is conducted, with here and there an exception,—especially their minister, so far as I have known,—have shown a willing disposition to clear Dr. Torsey and the faculty from all blame, and repeat the various charges and reports against my child.

My wife has belonged to that denomination about thirty years; and as the interest of that denomination is now to sustain their leading man at that institution, she sees that all her hard labor in taking care of their ministers and members at her home, and the funds given in that direction, are but of little account, when the reputation of one of their leading men is at stake. They have nothing to do to alleviate her sorrows, to heal the awful wound, to console her grief, to defend the character of her child, up to the time she was accused; no excuse to make for this one act of her life. They can repeat the charges against her, and insinuate that she had not been all right before; while they abound in excuses for those who managed this sad affair.

I will say to such, as Peter said, "God is no respecter of persons." To err is human; to forgive, divine. "By their fruit ye shall know them."

And now let me say to all, that, as you have the evidence, such as would be sustained in any court, as proof that Louise had lost at the college in the eleven weeks which she had boarded there this term, up to the time I took her trunk and other articles away, over sixty articles,—four to one of all they have ever accused her of having; and from the day when you shall come into possession of these facts, one and all, for the sake of truth and justice, when you hear repeated the charges against her whose tongue is silent in death, just say somebody had taken four articles of hers, to one of which they accuse her; and that embraces five pairs of cotton drawers, the last wearable pair she had; and that she rode away, and walked to the couch of death with none on, as she said, and which was proved by the discovery of her remains. And was there not some necessity for putting on others unmarked in their stead?

"I had no intention of stealing them; if mine had not come before the term was done, I should have left them in the wash."

O my God! where is the conscience of those who took, and now have, her last pair of common drawers, when they know she must have suffered intensely from cold for the want of them, as she lay dying on the cold earth through those chilly nights in May! God may forgive them and those who so wickedly pursue to disgrace her memory; I cannot, unless they show a different disposition than they have done.

There are many other articles lost, which we believe she had with her at the college; they are not named in Mrs. Green's sworn statement; not having positive personal knowledge, they are not mentioned; such as books, stockings, handkerchiefs, and various small articles; with a bank book, showing a deposit of eighteen dollars to her credit in a Boston Savings' Bank.

Some of the lost and sworn-to articles were plainly marked, — and somebody knows where they are. Where are all those sixty or more articles? Echo answers, — Where?

They at that college should forever be silent as to stealing, until they render some account of these lost articles belonging to my daughter. Why did they pursue L. to such extent to prove that she had, and to hunt up owners to claim, unmarked articles, when they will tell all, that they are not responsible for unmarked articles? And why did Miss Case, in violation of rule, put into the wash unmarked articles, and so readily claim and take from L. the same? And why did Mrs. Daggett, the next day after L. left, go into L.'s and Mary Chapman's room with Miss Hunton and others, and take up an unmarked article and suppose it belonged to others, who knew that article was there before Louise left? There are dark spots all the way along.

"Is there not a hole somewhere in that building where things disappear and are seen no more there"? as my wife told Mrs. Daggett, Nov. 8, 1866. Had we not lost enough there to be allowed to say that? We had borne and forborne the losses there in 1861, '62, '63, '64, and '65, in silence, for her sake, for fear of appearing small, and getting up a feeling against her. When we have borne all this without saying a word to them, it does seem too hard that no leniency should have been extended to our child!

As soon as we reached home with L.'s things, May 30, and found lots of her clothing and other articles missing, Mrs. Greene (as I was obliged to leave immediately to continue the search), wrote Mr. Daggett, and notified him of the things she had then missed, so that he could look them up before that term closed, when all the students were there. He made no reply; never answered her letter. At a later date she wrote Mr. Torsey that many of L.'s things were lost. Neither he nor Daggett, from that day to the present time, has written us a word of explanation about the same. In October, wanting some of L.'s books to send to Chestina, who was away to school, we wrote Miss Reed (as we could not get a word from those who Prof. Robinson says, "have nothing but pity for L.'s friends," that anything was there, or that they would ever try to look them up), and asked her if she would go to the college and see if she could find the two valuable books, and ask them if any other articles were there. Mrs. Daggett brought forward two books, —but not the ones we wrote for, — L.'s Adelphia pin, with her name plainly marked on the same, with some other articles, to the amount of, perhaps, in all, five dollars. These are none of the articles sworn to, by Mrs. Greene, as now lost. Why did Mrs. D. keep those articles from the last of May, until October, with L.'s name marked on some of them, when Mrs. Daggett admitted to Miss Reed, at this time, that she knew my wife had written for them, and asked them to look them up? Any mother would be very desirous to know all about the lost one's things, under such circumstances. I repeat, why did she keep them, and withhold all information? What means all this in my daughter's first, foremost, and fast accuser, — one who could call L., to her mother, an habitual thief, because, as she said, L. said she had been in the habit of taking unmarked articles, when hers were lost, to wear until hers came again? Mrs. Greene says to her, Nov. 8, when Mrs. D. said that L. had been putting drawers in the wash several weeks before, "Why did you not tell me when I was here nine days before she left?" Mrs. D. then distinctly said, in my presence, "We never mistrusted any kind of a thing until Monday night before she left Wednesday morning;" and as Mrs. G. was blaming them there for the way they treated L., and about the large amount of articles lost there, she said, "I know somebody is to blame; somebody knows where they are." Mrs. Daggett whined out, "I had rather bear the blame myself than have Dr. Torsey," and continued to say, "I have done nothing that I am sorry for, nothing but what I would do again."

Dr. Torsey tells Miss Reed, that he had no regrets when he went to Lewiston, and to the place where her remains were found. S. R. Bearce, who went with him, tells the same; that Torsey said, his conscience was clear; that he had done all he could to save her, or words to that effect; when he (Torsey) was the last person on earth who talked with her about her trouble, he leaving her alone, sending no one to her to comfort or assist her. As soon as he leaves, she takes off her jewelry, and some other valuables, hastily writes these words on a little scrap of paper, — "Heart breaking, dearly beloved, adieu," — then leaves the room and building, without saying a word to any one, hastily tries to see her sister, then takes the stage, flees from this man as from a tiger, and from the Hill; flees from class-mates, teachers, room-mate, and all her friends on earth, — alone, shunning everybody she knew, — goes to Lewiston and walks to the solitary forest, and to the couch of death, and there, with a broken heart, far from home and friends, in that lonely forest, with no hand to administer to her, with none to speak words of comfort, with no eye to pity, save the all-seeing eye of God, she lays herself down and dies. In four months and twenty days, her decayed form is discovered. Who on earth could have believed that

Torsey, who had been at the head of that school so long, had her under his control and care for five years, could have been so self-righteous, and so self-conceited, or hard-hearted, as to believe that it was not possible that he had made some mistake, neglected some duty, or in some way, when the sad result was known, had failed to do all he could then have wished he had done, or that if he had done differently, this awful result could have been avoided? Who, under all the circumstances, could feel that his conscience was clear, — that they could or would not have done differently if they had known the sad result? Do the public believe their bold assertions? If so, God pity them! and parents should be cautious how they trust their children in their hands.

I do not know that I should doubt their assertions, after the manner they received us in that faculty meeting, and the letters I have received from Torsey, and what he said to Mrs. G., the cool way and manner of their arguments and appearances; when Prof. Morse read her class-letter so coolly, not the slightest emotions perceptible by any except one or two lady teachers. I do not know about such persons having any conscience. I scarcely ever saw a stranger read that letter without shedding tears. The very recital of the circumstances of her leaving to strangers, when I was looking for her, would often cause a sympathetic tear, while the leading members of that faculty could so coolly treat us in our greatest distress. Torsey tried, in that meeting, to find out what we were going to say about her loss; and when we were accusing him of prejudice and injustice, he stamped his foot on the floor, and tried to stop us with this show of authority, or to stamp us down. If he would thus attempt to exercise his authority over us, we may well judge how he would be likely to treat our child if she made any attempt to defend herself.

Torsey will not admit that she was not just herself, but tells Roscoe Smith, as he (Smith) says two weeks after L. had gone, that if either was crazy, it was her mother. I can only say to those self-righteous people, who have no regrets, and would do the same again under like circumstances, that they very much resemble a certain sect whom, in the days of Christ, he called Pharisees.

Where is the evidence that he was kind to her, or tried to make this trouble look favorable to her? He says he was kind to her. I have no evidence of that; but there *is* evidence clear to my mind that he knew she was not fully in her right mind, when he says he told her if she did go, to let her sister make all the arrangements. What does this mean? Why attempt to put her under that much younger sister, who was a stranger there compared to this old student, if he believed her fully sane? Facts *will* creep out.

If Torsey should say the school knew it before he did, would that help the case? Should the next in authority — Miss Case, the preceptress, and Mrs. Daggett — proceed in the examination, without his knowledge, when he was there, and then let all be known to the school, before he knew it? No one would believe that, after we have proved that Miss Case and Mrs. D. went into his part of the house before entering Miss Reed and Chestina's room the day before L. left. One more point. Who believes, if this had been Prof. Perley's daughter, or a favorite of Torsey, that he could and would not have found some way to have kept the matter private, and from the school, — saved her character and life? I have not a shadow of doubt that nothing but the will was wanting to have done that in poor Louise's case.

A student writes me, under date of March 24, 1867. With other things, he says, "I cannot state facts, that is, positive evidence; but yet, I am assured in my own mind that favoritism and partiality did exist, arising not only from sectarian motives, but other more trivial, but not less culpable considerations. I say this in no spirit of animosity or fancied injustice done me, for I have none, but as an unprejudiced observer; was a member of the school five terms, and think I have drawn my conclusions rightly."

Another student writes Mrs. Greene, under date March 1, 1867. Among other things, she says: "I lost a pair of good stockings. I think I lost those the last week of the spring term. Mrs. Daggett did not know where they went to, and I am sure I don't. Nearly all the girls lost more or less that they put into the wash. I never could understand why there need to be so many things lost. Poor Louise! how much she must have suffered? I have often thought what my feelings must have been under similar circumstances. God only knows her feelings, for I think no one else can. It was very hard that she remained alone the night before she left. The girls felt badly about it, but did not know it till the next morning."

God and those who hold the skeleton keys only know — I do not — how much their skeleton keys had to do about their finding out her real sentiments or feelings towards them, by examining her private correspondence, in her room, in her absence!

From one of her class I have a letter under date of December, 1866, from which I make the following extract: "I dare not judge the teachers of intentional wrong, though that some great wrong has been done I think none will deny.

"It is very strange where so many of Louise's things are. There are things taken as supposed every term by the help, and was last term at the close. Louise was very much loved by the students, with but very few exceptions. I think no one will deny that. I always loved her even before I knew her well, and since I've known her intimately I've counted her among my dearest friends. Louise was a *true* friend, and had the kindest, most sympathizing heart of any girl I knew. We always sought her in trouble or sorrow. Her life was full of sympathy and care for those around her."

In another letter from an old student, she says, writing to Mrs. Greene from Kent's Hill, October 7, 1866: "I talked with Mary Chapman: she says it makes her mad to hear a word said against Louise, and she did not think she had any evil intentions, only was careless about looking after her own clothing." (This writer continues:) "I cannot see why any one should try to hurt Louise's character, for she was very particular in regard to her gentleman associates. She always selected those who had the best standing in school. I have heard *that* repeated time and again, by those that were well acquainted with her. She is wronged when it is said of her she had not an unspotted character. Do not think I say these things because I am writing to you; it is what I say to all, and what I sincerely believe."

Mary Chapman writes me, from which I make the following extract. Speaking of Louise before her body was found: "I pity her from the bottom of my heart, and gladly, oh, so gladly! would I again take her into my confidence and love her as before. I always treated her as a sister; in fact, she took the place of one to me, and a kind and good one she was."

Do students go, or are they sent, to Kent's Hill to build up that religious denomination? This may be the object for which some are sent there, but it is no part of the purpose for which many students go there. To get an education is the great object; this is what the State has endowed colleges and academies for. This institution has received large amounts in land and money from the State. In 1827, it received one half township of land, and subsequently, at seven different times, it has received from the State eighteen thousand six hundred dollars. Who gets the benefits of this more than twenty thousand dollars from the people of the State? Do the students get the benefit of it? Nothing but the chance to attend that school by paying well for all they get there. Does not this twenty thousand dollars put them under some obligations to the public to guard, protect, and take good care of all the students who are entrusted to their care? and no artifice or dodge of Dr. T. will excuse him by saying a student is of age. That faculty is under every obligation, legal, moral, and religious, to impartially teach, protect, and defend the rights of every student, of whatever name age, sect, or color, whom they have or shall receive into their school; and he who for any cause, holding such a responsible position, allows his prejudice to prevent an impartial performance of all his duties, has forfeited all claim to public confidence, or the respect of individuals.

Will Dr. T. yet say that he left it to her about leaving? It looks as though he means to say that by and by, by what he wrote me in October 1866: "I spoke only at any time of her leaving, when she had decided to go home." All who know that man and the authority he exercises on the Hill (and L. knew it well), know he is not in the habit of leaving much to the student to decide; no, not he, by no means; he is one whose actions show that he believes he was born to command, and all the right students have is to obey. In proof of this I will here let some students speak for themselves, and here I would call the attention of that wise and knowing committee of students, to see how much they knew what their Rev. H. P. Torsey, LL. D., the President, had or had not done. They seem to think, as it looks to me in their article of about two-thirds of a column in the *Farmer*, that the repeating of the title President, which they have done *ten* times in that communication, with Rev. and LL. D. sometimes attached, would be a clincher, and the public must take all they have resolved and said to clear Torsey, as true; as they would believe him to be a mighty big and powerful man.

From a letter to me from a student dated May 7, 1867, I make the following extracts: —

"Your daughter was a kind friend of mine during my stay at Kent's Hill, and her conduct towards all exemplary. During a recitation in reading under Prof. Torsey, I laughed at something the professor said, and another student laughed, too. Prof. Torsey said, 'Stop laughing immediately,' and we could not. Instead of correcting us as a gentleman, for I grant we did wrong, not intending it for impudence but merely because we could not control ourselves, he took the other student (she gives her name) by the ear and pulled her to a front seat, and took the back of the book and knocked me in the face with it several times; this he did before a class of ladies and gentlemen. He never spoke one kind word to me during my stay; his only spirit towards me was a domineering one. He governed by fear, not by love. This the other student certainly will tell you was done, if she says anything about it;" and then she gives me the reason why she thinks the other student might not like to say anything about the matter. She then continues and says: "But there is a just God, who will certainly bring the one who caused your grief to a higher tribunal than an earthly one." She offers to make oath to the truth of this statement.

In another letter, dated June 19, 1867, the writer says: "I think Mr. Torsey is a good teacher, as far as his scholarship extends; and, were it not for his strong prejudices, he would be a good disciplinarian. He is a man to be feared more than respected. He has a faculty of appearing very religious, and will make a favorable impression upon a man who sees but one side of him. But the man who knows him as thoroughly as I know him will not be disposed to speak of him in favorable terms. Mr. Torsey may be a Christian, but I have for years prayed that I might have a different kind of religion. The seminary folks' meeting held at the seminary, and the action there taken did not change my mind at all about the matter. I was with them so long, that I understand how those meetings are got up. The *hand* that moves the whole thing is not seen by the undiscerning."

I have just received a letter, dated July 22, 1867, in which the writer says: "I lost my wallet with its contents the latter part of the spring term. It was taken out of my room (which was left unlocked) some time during the night. I have not found out anything about it yet. The wallet contained about $700 in money. I remember at the time hearing of a number of the students who lost money and other articles."

This student, at the time he lost his money, was boarding in the college building. It is a well-known fact, when they choose to keep those things private, that they have a good faculty to do so; hence the school and the public know but very little about this student, or Miss Grover losing money, or the other students losing money and other articles, as this student says, at that term.

In another letter, dated June, 1867, an old student, — one who has been there for years, and had boarded in the college; a student of good sound judgment; one who had as good a chance as any to judge correctly; who was there when L. left, — says: "Dr. Torsey's authority in the school, I think, is unlimited. But this is my opinion, and, I think, is the opinion of nearly every student of the Hill, that whatever measure Dr. Torsey thought best to adopt, the faculty would unhesitatingly agree with him. As to what course they would have pursued in regard to Louise, if she had remained, I am not prepared to say, further than this, — I do not think they would have allowed her to graduate."

I have quoted from this letter to show what everybody conversant on the Hill knows to be true (although Torsey may say the trustees voted the diplomas; he may say this, that, or the other for an excuse that he did not know what the faculty would do), that Torsey's power is unlimited, in or out of the school, in regard to everything pertaining to the whole arrangement. He had the whole power in his own hands, and could and did do just as he pleased with my poor girl. Had he adopted a course which would have saved her, it would have been sanctioned and agreed to by the other members of the faculty.

At the bottom of one of the letters from which I have made quotations I find the following: —

"P. S. — A *sly*, *subtle*, *vindictive* person can do almost anything to *carry* his *point*, under the *cloak* of religion, and, at the same time, be sustained by a clique or sect."

This is exactly my opinion of the man; and, if my poor girl was living, she would say that his treatment of her had proved him to be such a man. Having quoted largely from letters and other writings, without giving the writers' names, in most cases unnecessary to the public, I wish for all who shall read it, fully to understand that I have, in every case, quoted the exact language of all, both letters and other writings; and that I have and shall keep each and all on file; and that I have not made a quotation from a single letter marked private or confidential.

Will Dr. T., or any who dealt with her, yet come out openly and attack her previous good character? It would seem rather strange and incredible for Torsey, or any other member of the faculty, the steward or his wife, at this late day, to make any such attempt; when, during all those five years, with my other three daughters, who have been there from one to two terms each, while I or Mrs. Greene have been on the Hill, to take them to, from, and to see to them there, from six to ten times yearly, stopping from one to three days each, — and one time Mrs. G. was there over three weeks, during the sickness of two of the girls, — no complaint had ever reached us from Torsey, any other member of the faculty, the boarding-master or his wife, that Louise or the other girls had been remiss in lessons, disobeying rules of the school, or in any way that they had behaved unbecoming as students at their school. No, not a word of complaint had ever reached us from them by any other person or student but what all four of our girls were well-behaved at the Hill, until twelve o'clock at night, May 23, 1866, and, like a thunderbolt, that report struck us to the heart! None can tell the awful shock but those who received it. It will ill become them 'at this late day' to complain to the public, while during those five years they could find nothing worthy of the least complaint to her parents, who should have been informed and consulted at the time if she was at fault. In view of all the evidence of her good standing at home and elsewhere, and the absence of any complaints against her up to this time, I will let the public draw their own conclusions, only saying, that, although they tried to make her account for all the little things lost during the term up to the time she left, they cannot hold her responsible for Mrs. Grover's money, which they pursued and took from Miss M.; also, the wallet and money of Mr. Gower, a student; a music-book, and lots of hats, and other things, which were lost there soon after Louise left.

Dr. Torsey admits to us in that faculty meeting one *fact*, which all who knew her will endorse, when he says, "Your daughter, although in rags, with her open and frank countenance, and her lady-like manners, will find friends wherever she goes; any one will take her in" (he should have excepted himself). This shows at once that deception or dishonesty was no part of her nature. It is not strange, therefore, that she should be misunderstood and misjudged by those who we believe have practised deception, and understood that art so long and well. An eminent writer has said, "What the world wants is not honesty, but acquiescence." Without fully subscribing to that sentiment, that idea has been plainly illustrated, I think, on Kent's Hill. Acquiescence in the decision and opinions of the faculty would have covered a multitude of sins.

Louise knew full well their power and disposition to crush all who should attempt to say anything in palliation or excuse for her, as she wrote to her sister, "It will be useless for you to say anything in excuse or palliation; it will break you down; bend beneath it." She foresaw the course they would pursue towards her sister if she tried to defend her; she knew how they had pursued her about hearsays and little things. She would, doubtless, if she could, say to her parents, for any defence you may make for me, that faculty will pursue, harass, and try to break you down. It has been said that the article written by one of the officiating clergymen at her funeral, who was assisted by a prominent citizen of Peru, and published in the "Loyal Sunrise" of Nov. 23, 1866, was untrue, and the position therein assumed, in saying "her enemies were relentless," was wrong. I can only say that those gentlemen had access to all the communications between Dr. T., myself, Louise, her writings, and various letters from her class, and other students, and that they came to the conclusion that such a course as all this indicated towards her and her family did not look like the actions of friends. I will state, for the information of the faculty, trustees, and that committee of students, that neither I nor any member of my family knew anything about the article that appeared in the "Sunrise" of January 11, 1867.

Let me recapitulate and sum up some of their proceedings, and the treatment Louise, her sister, and her parents have received at the hands of this faculty and those under them, and then judge whether this is the action of friends or enemies.

Monday night they say something to her about the clothing. Tuesday Mrs. Daggett and Miss Case enter, unbeknown, and search their room, then go into an examination. She explains. They closely search and open all her things; that little fancy box or trunk, holding about a quart, could not be exempted. They, when exhausted in their accusations, call in Mr. Daggett to assist them. She frankly tells them all the whole truth, as she says in her class letter: "I told them the truth as near as I could in my distracted state of mind." She did not deny a word, — refunds. But these, some say, friends were not content; they must disgrace her sister, also. They proceed up to and into Dr. T.'s part of his house (as I suppose, to report progress, and to get further instructions), then enter Chestina's and Miss Reed's room. They tell her L.'s confession and all, represent that she had lots of marked and unmarked articles in her room, trunk, and drawer, and say what an awful thing it is; then ask to, and search her trunk and all her things. Are they content? Not yet. They ask her if there is not another trunk kept there. Was this not trying to make them or L. account for all the articles lost at this term? Was this like the action of friends to my girls, without knowledge to me, and without authority, to enter Miss Reed's and my daughter's room, — a room as sacred to them; a room where they had rights as well as you, kind reader, have in your own quiet domicile, where no ruthless hand has a right, without due process of law, to enter and overhaul at will? They may say that they asked leave of these students to do this, that, or the other thing. What students would dare to deny under such circumstances? They find nothing, but tell her sister all in the worst form. Mr. Chandler, who comes home with C. that night, knows it all in an exaggerated form, as told by Miss Case and D. Mr. Swagles, a boarder with Dr. T., tells L. he knows all, Wednesday, on the stage. They leave her alone that night, although Miss Daggett and three lady teachers board in the same building. They have no friendly word to say to her, no advice to give. They do not approach her lonely room to see if she does not desire some friendly act, some friend sent for to read or pray with her. They all knew she was in trouble. Was it because they were afraid they should displease Dr. T., or was it, as he said, because "she was under censure"? Would it disgrace them? Do the teachings of Christ appear in those professed followers? She, as it were, with her brain on fire, walks her lonely room through that night. She writes in her letter the next day: "I tried to read my Bible last night, but could not," thus showing a partial derangement, a wretched state of mind. Does this look like the action of Christians or friends in those who had known her so long? Torsey takes her alone the next morning, and has a long conversation with her. He appeals to her to know what she wants done. She says: "I want it kept from the school, — to stay and graduate." He tells her the school knew it; that she had better leave that day. Will he deny this? He tells Miss Reed so, and that L. further said, "If she could not graduate, there was no future for her." He tells Chestina "it would not have been best for her to have gone on to the stage," etc. If he had not desired her to leave, or if he had wanted her to have graduated or been willing for her to, would he have answered Chestina as he did? Would he have said it would not have been best for her to have gone on to the stage? She would have been pointed out as the girl that stole. He could not help letting it out to her sister that he meant everybody should know her confession about the money. If he had desired her to have stopped and graduated, his answer to C. would have been: Yes; she could have graduated. I wanted her to, and if we can get her back, she can now. In two weeks after she left, he tells Roscoe Smith, who lived then near me, as he (Smith) tells me in the presence of others, that Torsey told him in presence of others, that when L. made the request to have it kept from the school, and she stay and graduate, he told her the school knew it. She writes soon as she leaves the Hill, after failing to see her sister before she left, that Dr. Torsey "informed me this: that I had better leave to-day. 'Not expulsion,' he said; 'we won't call it that; but I advise you to go home.' Practically, is amounts to the same thing, however. How I feel, God only knows; you never can," etc. Mr. Smith further said that Dr. T. told him and others, at the time above referred to (he then pretended to think she was living), all about her confession, and other things in that last and private conversation, and further said if either was crazy, it was her mother. With the letters he has written me, does the reader see any friendly hand in all those proceedings? Will any parent believe for a moment, if this was their case, their child, that all those proceedings were the acts of friends? Would friends have reported her private confession to disgrace her? She had done all she could to deserve forbearance. In *God's* name were they not doing all they could to chagrin and mortify her sister in the house of the principal of this school, — to disappoint, distract, and break the heart of L.? Does that long string of written misrepresentations of Professor Robinson, which he calls *facts*, look like the actions of a friend? He says: "At the request of the faculty Mr. Torsey called to see Miss G. and talk with her about the matter." He does not say why or what they requested him to see or talk with her about. Again he says: "No intimation was given her that she must leave the school, — that she could not graduate. Mr. Torsey expressly said to her that if she left, it would not be on account of any action of the faculty." (What whoppers!) Does any one believe she was seeking to leave in disgrace? See the sworn statements of Miss Reed, C. S. Greene, Louise's letter, Mr. Smith's statement. Query: For what did the faculty request T. to call to see L.? She had confessed, explained all, refunded the money. She had but two weeks longer to remain. She was feeling bad enough. If she was the bad girl they now would have people believe, did they expect to reform her in two weeks, if no intimation was to be given her about leaving, or that she could not graduate? I repeat, why did the faculty request him to call and talk with her about the matter? Oh, could she speak, then we should know what further he said to her, — what the faculty sent him to her for other than advising her to leave that day, and saying "we won't call it expulsion." (It is expulsion, but I will deceive, dissemble, withhold the real fact, won't call it what it is, what you and I understand it to be.) Why is all this prevarication? All this does not look like the actions of friends. To me and to my family it looks like the doings of some unfriendly hands, enemies, and relentless ones, too. Would a friend have written me as Dr. T. did, June 30, 1866, — not answering my one question, but putting a half dozen insulting questions to me, and then adding this threat, "Such reports as these may *oblige* us to state the facts publicly"?

Again he writes me, July 11, 1866, again asking questions about flying reports of what he has heard that I and Mrs. Greene have said to certain persons, and then adds, "You know she stole money and can find no one that will tell you I ever brought the matter before the school." And then advising a double lawsuit in those words, "By bringing a case of libel or slander, followed on our part by a prosecution for malicious prosecution and for slander." Had I given him any cause for those insulting letters? The reader can judge, as I have laid before them every letter and word I have written him since L. left, they being only two in all; and I have kept a copy of all the letters I have written him since Louise first went to that school. I know whereof I speak, and that I have not given him cause thus to insult and abuse me. Would a friend at this time, when I had spent five weeks from home in this sad and fruitless search to find any reliable trace of our child; my wife prostrate after she makes one trip with me, and, despairing of ever finding her, takes her bed; my children in the greatest distress and commotion watch for some tidings of the missing one, they needing all my care; but duty and anxiety for the lost one kept me away as long as a possible chance or hope remained. Yet, on two occasions when I did reach home, I found those letters before named, from this pompous, bigoted, overbearing, and heartless man. Was this sympathy, or was it not to *awe* me into silence at the fear of his publicly disgracing my once lovely girl who had fled in dismay before his power? Judge ye which. Would a friend have disregarded the warning of Miss Reed and Chestina about her probable destruction, and the earnest wish to have some one pursue her to Lewiston, as they had requested Harriman to do? Why did this head man, — the only one to order and direct on the Hill — parley, hesitate, argue and thus try to quiet their fears; why put it off from twelve to six o'clock, after he knew where and how she had gone? (I know he has said he thought best to wait until after the stage returned from the depot, at four, to see if the conductor could tell whether she stopped at L. or not.) This would be very uncertain, — a most miserable excuse for delay. She should have been pursued regardless of where she should stop. Would he have thus delayed if it had been his own child? Although I cannot recall the past or recover our daughter, whom we took so pure, so innocent, in 1861 to Kent's Hill and put under the charge and protection of this "Rev. H. P. Torsey, LL.D., the President" of that religious institution, should we — after the long years we kept her there, after her suffering and death, under the circumstances of this sad case, with the disposition those who dealt with her show to disgrace her memory and to injure the feelings of parents and friends,— should we bear it all, and the thousand misrepresentations of what she was guilty go uncorrected? I believe it to be a duty from which I cannot escape,— a duty I owe to her memory, to myself and family, to her numerous friend, and to the public,— to state all the facts of this case which have come to my knowledge, and leave all to judge whether my daughter and family have been fairly used by those who control that institution. I, as I told Torsey in that faculty meeting, should not dare to trust another child to his care.

When we consider how liable the young are to step from the strict path of rectitude, and know not how great the temptation may be, if for the first offence, for five dollars (God only knows the real cause why it was done), frank acknowledgment and private restoration are made, should they make such woful work, such hasty reports, pursue to such extent, give her such advice, neglect her, and delay to notify her friends till too late to save her, till she had time to get beyond our reach? When we consider how many in early life and some in mature years have done something or caused others to do as bad; as the taking of five dollars, and all has been quietly kept with those alone who necessarily knew it, — they being usually well-disposed persons, who have in after life made first-rate men and women, have been an ornament to society and done much good in the world; whereas exposure might have ruined them forever; — surely " kind words can never die," and may be productive of much good. Was there any good reason if all was true, for putting the worst construction upon this, her first offence? Should they not have used every means to keep the matter private, made the best of it, allowed her to graduate, or at least quietly and immediately notified her friends before intimating to her what the result would be? She had a right to be heard by counsel; we had rights and should have been notified early in the trouble. I had paid them money enough to put them under some obligations; they owed some consideration to so old a student (of five years). She had lost enough there to have entitled her to some forbearance. They may say that they could not have kept it from the school; they seem to have power to keep the taking of money and other articles by other students quite still. Who took Mrs. Grover's ten dollars and five cents? But few knew it, and less know who took thirty dollars, the hats, and music-book since L. left. They have a good faculty to keep what they choose from the school and the public. How much have they said about those sixty articles that Louise lost at the last term at the college? In God's name do not, for the sake of truth and justice, ever again represent that L. confessed in her letter that she stole even unmarked articles of clothing, when she distinctly in her letter to her sister says: "I had no intention of stealing them; for every article I took I had lost one in the wash, and put those on in their stead, expecting before the term was done to find my own. There was some sort of necessity for this. For instance, I came to the college with three or four good whole drawers; to day as I ride away I have none. Was it so strange that I should put on others also unmarked in their stead?" In her class letter referring to the unmarked articles she says: "But if my own garments had not come by the close of the term, I should have left those where I got them, in the wash." She further says: "I can feel myself guilty of but one crime, the taking of the five dollars." There is no confession of stealing clothes at all. What a reward for her frank confession did she receive by those who dealt with her! Here I wish to put a question to the good judgment and common sense of all. If my girl had been a pilfering, thieving person, or a loose character, one who had been caught in mean things, had got herself out, by deception or otherwise, of dirty scrapes, would she have laid this so much to heart, take so much blame to herself, and think she had disgraced herself and friends, think her parents and friends would not forgive and be willing to receive her; that the Saviour was an iron door to her, shut and bolted; that God would not hear or forgive her in this or the world to come? And was not Miss Case too bad in trying to impress upon her the enormity of the crime, and was not Torsey trying to do the same thing, when he, as he writes me, says, "My talk with her was about going to God and to you with the whole matter"? Again he writes: "I had a long conversation with her the morning she left, and urged upon her two things, first, that she go to Jesus with the whole matter, making this sad event the beginning of a humble, earnest Christian life; and second, that she go at once to her father and mother, telling them all." Now I appeal (to her confused and distracted mind) if this was not making her believe that she had committed so terrible a crime as to get down to a mere nothing before God and her parents to ask pardon, and that she leave the school in disgrace, and go at once to her father and mother telling them all; as though she had committed a heinous offence, a great crime, so much so, that she must go at once to them. How could she graduate? No delay would answer. If this was necessary, how do you suppose she thought he, Torsey, looked upon her crimes? This in my opinion was just what he meant, and did bring her to see herself when he advised her to leave, and how much mercy do you suppose she could expect from him? Do you wonder that she writes, "heart breaking" as he left her?

One has asked, what reason existed why they should desire to disgrace her, to send her away, and thus rob themselves of one of their best scholars at the approaching commencement? I answer, what good reason had he to refuse her reasonable request, and turn her out of his house with threats? Did he give her or me a sufficient reason? Did it not plainly show that it was at least in part because he disliked her friend, who had left his school, and, as Louise writes, because she and her folks were not right on the goose? It is clear to me that he was carrying into execution his threat, "if she should do anything that looked like a wilful violation of any rule, she could expect but little forbearance from the faculty." Yes, that man and this faculty knew that she was not with them heart and soul as he expressed it; that after she graduated, not by word or pen would they receive from her aught but condemnation of the narrow and bigoted course they had pursued towards her and others who did not think as they did, and that this faculty was human and liable to err. Disgrace would destroy her influence. Her talent for writing they might have feared.

In reply to the report and misstatements made by A. J. Blethen, E. M. Smith, A. W. Waterhouse, Margie Houschild, Nellie A. Wing, and Mary E. Deering, acting as and purporting to be a committee of students chosen May 6, 1867, at a chapel exercise, after they had requested their teachers to withdraw; I say to this committee and to the public that, after a careful perusal of this pamphlet, they will find that I have produced evidence and circumstances which will satisfy the impartial reader that most of the positions assumed in their preamble and resolves, and the statement therein made by this committee are refuted and shown to be untrue, while they were putting them before the public as "facts," of which they say, "many of us were personally acquainted with the circumstances;" when in fact they did not have any personal knowledge of what they state. They go on to assert what was "utterly false," and with great boldness resolve what "is truthful." The reader will see that the doings of these students were a short time before the graduation of some of them, and to get into the good graces of this faculty, of which Torsey is chief, — and in fact as many students have expressed it, — Dr. T. is the faculty. I know and have seen enough to believe those students have it about right. Favoritism had much to do I believe in their overmuch zeal to acquit and puff Dr. T., while they make up such a string of misstatements against an old school-mate, one whose reputation and standing was as good as their own for five long years at that school, and send them broadcast over the State to disgrace her memory, and injure the feeling of her friends, while she sleeps in death and can make no reply. Is not Dr. Torsey able to make his own defence? The public may think it would have been as well to have let the faculty have had all the honor of pursuing their dead pupil. Torsey and others may say they knew nothing of this action of the students, he being away, etc. But I know this old angler so well, who knows how to throw his line and cover the hook, that I believe he knew just what would be done in his absence and how it would be accomplished. There are always enough who wish for favors to keep him quietly posted. Who believes that the other teachers did not know what was to be done when they left the hall? What right had students to remain after service if the cause was not known to, and permission given by the teachers? On reception of the action of this committee through the public journals, I addressed the following note to each member of this committee, under date of June 7, 1867, addressing each respectfully as follows: —

"As you appear before the public as one of the committee who have made numerous statements in regard to my daughter's leaving the college at Kent's Hill, and as you state them to be *facts*, and that you were personally acquainted with the circumstances, and that you do so to correct false and groundless statements, please inform me what personal knowledge you have of what Messrs. Torsey, Daggett, his wife, and Miss Case said or did to Louise, or what they did not do or say?

"Please state how you know that the crime was not known to any member of the faculty, until many of those otherwise connected with the school knew it; and that Torsey notified me to be in Lewiston before any morning train left; that the teachers did not know nothing of the matter until others were in possession of every circumstance; that, by the President, never has a single act of unkindness been manifested towards *any* student; and that Louise was not expelled from the school?

"Yours, respectfully,

"JONAS GREENE."

Is there anything disrespectful in this letter? Certainly not, the reader will say; and believing, as I do, that three-fourths of their statements were entirely false (and knowing some of them to be so), that this was a wicked and uncalled-for attack on our dead child, I was under no obligations to write them; but as I did not know but some one of this committee might be in possession of one *fact*, at least, of what they state they had knowledge of, and as I have spared no pains to obtain every fact possible, being very desirous of getting at the whole truth. As there was one ungrammatical sentence in those letters, my friend, to whom I showed them, and pointed out this sentence, and the reason why I put it in, will smile to see how one of those sprigs of learning, Mr. A. J. Blethen, for the reason that he could not answer any of my questions, he having assisted in publishing as facts that which he knew nothing about, snapped at this bait and for *his* answer, wrote over the top of my letter these words, — "Should advise a careful perusal of English grammar," and returned it to me, evidently as an insult. He has put forth statements as facts, and could not give me a civil answer; how does he know a single one of them to be true?

I advise him, and the other four members of this committee, who have made no reply to my anxious but respectful request, to let Dr. Torsey, and the others who are implicated in this sad affair, take care of their own reputation, while he and his associates had better be attending to their own business. Modesty should have prevented her own sex, at least from appearing before the public to disparage her memory, and wound the feelings of her friends.

From A. W. Waterhouse, one of this committee, I received a respectful note, but entirely failing to answer any of my questions. He says: —

"With regard to statements made by the committee, of which I was a member, I will simply say, we endeavored to state the simple truth; nothing more, nothing less. As to explanations, which you ask, I refer you to the statements as printed. You cannot blame the students and friends of Dr. Torsey for wishing to have a fair statement of the case before the public."

What fair statement have you spread broadcast over the State? Simply this. You have repeated Torsey's and the others' statements to clear themselves, without asking or trying to find out a single word of what the friends of Louise knew or had to say in her defence. Not a word as to his or their knowledge does this member of *this* committee give me as to how they know what they published as *facts*, to be true. He does not answer one of my questions, but refers me to what they have printed; as much as to say, — you must take what we have said as true because Dr. T. has told us so! Does that make a clear case for the party implicated to say he is innocent?

They quote from L.'s letter with a relish where it tells against her; while nothing is said about any part of the letter where "H. P. Torsey, LL. D., the President," is implicated!

The public will at once see where *they* desire the whole blame to rest. As I have before said, fear or favoritism predominates on the Hill, and their reward came speedily, as this committee of six took one-third of all the prizes awarded to that whole school at their closing exhibition. From the other four members, I got no reply.

As I have spoken of a certain denomination usually taking sides with the faculty, and showing a great desire to apologize and to clear them from blame (no doubt but what there are many exceptions), let me give the reader a sample how some of their leading members have met this sad case.

In October last, while I was at Lewiston for the remains of my daughter soon after they were discovered, and there waiting for the coroner to return, as he was absent, — as I intended to have a *post mortem* examination, to ascertain the immediate cause of her death, — while I was slowly pacing the sidewalks in sad and solemn thought, a stranger approached, and asked a question or two, and then said, "Is this Mr. Greene, of Peru, who has lost a daughter?" And on receiving an answer in the affirmative, he said, in substance, "I am one who do not visit the taverns or stores, much; I usually stay at home; but have heard that much has been said about your daughter's leaving the school at Kent's Hill; and many are disposed to blame Dr. Torsey very much, while others may think differently. But I am one who wishes to see justice done, — do not take sides or part in street controversies."

Thus he continued in a cool, sober strain, for some time, I making but little reply, as I was feeling very bad. But thinks I, who is this cool, fair-talking stranger? He soon said, "We are to have an investigation, and if T. is to blame, let it be known; let him take the consequences; if otherwise, let him be acquitted; let justice be done, and have the matter cleared up;" or words to that effect.

I began to think that all this fair talk meant something. Just as we were about to part, I looked at him and said, "Sir, although a stranger, I hope you are willing that justice shall be done to the memory of my poor, dead girl?"

He said, "Certainly," or words to that amount.

As we were passing along, he said, "I might as well say, that I am one of the trustees of that institution. My name is S. R. Bearce, of this place."

In a moment I thought I could see the whole length and breadth of him. I knew just where he would end, if this conversation was continued. I knew naught of him; but knew he must be a Methodist. He talked quite freely. I asked him some questions about the trustees.

I said, "Then Torsey is there by your (the trustees) authority?"

"Yes," was his reply.

"You control the whole matter, — do you?" (Meaning the general management and supervision of that institution.)

His answer was, "That is the purport, or our right; but we leave most all to Dr. Torsey. We do not have much to do, except in such a matter as this." (Meaning the investigation spoken of by him, I suppose.)

I asked him, — "when they proposed to investigate the matter?"

"Oh!" says he, "when you have the inquest." And said, "I see by the paper that you are to have it to-day; and I have *written* (he did not say he had sent for him) Torsey, and he will be here by noon to-day."

As we parted, thought I, "He was not a very disinterested stranger; and how did he know whom the coroner will see cause to summon before him as witnesses?"

The coroner did not arrive that day; but those interested Kent's Hillers (who never went one mile to my knowledge, out of their way; no, not one of them, to save my child, or in any way ever offered to assist me to find her) did come. Torsey, Mr. Daggett and his wife (and no doubt, if Miss Case had not gone home to New York, she would have come also) were prompt, and on hand, to testify and tell their story to clear themselves, without being called by the proper authorities willing witnesses in their own defence. A little more modesty would have made them appear as well.

I waited until the next day (Thursday), and, as the coroner had not arrived, and as the time was fixed for the funeral on Sunday, and there was much to be done at home to carry out the arrangements, I was obliged to take her remains home, where I arrived with them on Friday evening.

On Thursday forenoon, this sage and fair-talking S. R. Bearce, came into my brother's saloon in Auburn, and asked about the inquest, and said, "The coroner has got home" (which was not true), and said, "Torsey was there, but must go home at noon." My brother, his wife, and some others were present.

Mr. Bearce, my brother, and his wife began to talk about the cause and death of L. (I say but very little.) He (Bearce) again began in a seeming fair argument; but, as my brother's wife said something in Louise's defence, he (B.) then went on, stated the case, argued, and cleared T., in about two minutes, from all blame. He did not then, or at the other long interview on the street, ask me a single question, as to what I or my family knew of this sad case.

The reader can see from whom he desired and did get his information, or how much he cared about "justice being done."

On his leaving the saloon, my brother, who was a stranger to him, says, — "That is the man who so unceremoniously snatched that memoranda book out of my hands the other day, when I, with four others of L.'s uncles and aunts had just arrived at the spot where the remains of L. lay, and were trying to identify her. I had just taken this little book from her reticule, and was looking it over for that purpose."

At a later period, I learned that this man sent a team post-haste through to Kent's Hill (where it arrived at midnight), to notify Torsey. This shows the great interest taken, when the reputation of Dr. Torsey, the school, and denomination is at stake.

The public have seen in many of the papers of this State, the following statement, after the account of the anniversary exercises at Kent's Hill, June 5th and 6th, 1867: "By request of Dr. Torsey the trustees made a thorough investigation as to the conduct of the faculty in the case of the late Miss M. Louise Greene, and, as the result, they adopted resolutions and put them on file, entirely exonerating Dr. Torsey and the faculty from all blame, and fully approving their course." Mark well the first point in this statement: " by *request of Dr. T.*" Then it was not the trustees who instigated this examination. He desired to get before a committee of the trustees, and, with a long, sanctimonious face, tell his story, and, backed by his special friends, he thought he could make them believe he was not to blame. He well knew I was not fool enough to appear at such a time and place before so one-sided a tribunal.

As Dr. T. and the faculty, by this published statement, stand fully acquitted, and the trustees' committee are made to say they fully approve their course, the public are not informed how this was done. I owe to the memory of the dead, to myself and family, to show how this was accomplished; how "full and searching an investigation" (as one paper reports this matter) could have taken place.

On the 27th of May, 1867, I received a letter from F. A. Robinson, informing me that there would be a meeting of the trustees of that institution, June 5th, at ten o'clock A. M., "at which time the course of the faculty with reference to your daughter will be investigated by a committee chosen for that purpose. The faculty invite you to be present, and to prefer any charges you have to make against them, or to make any statement you wish to present."

To which I replied, May 28, as follows: —

"Prof. Robinson: Sir, — Yours of the 28th is received and contents noticed. You name the time but not the place of the meeting of the trustees. From whom and by whom are the investigating committee to be chosen?"

To which he replied, May 29, as follows: "The place of holding the meeting is in the seminary building, Kent's Hill. The committee will be of the trustees, and, of course, appointed by them. At an informal meeting held at Bath a few weeks since, the gentlemen were indicated to constitute the committee." He gave the names of five of the trustees as that committee.

On the receipt of this, I, May 31, answered as follows: "On the receipt of yours of the 27th, inviting me to an investigation of the course of the faculty in reference to my daughter, in answer to my inquiries of the 28th inst., asking you from whom and by whom are the investigating committee to be chosen, I never was more surprised in my life, than, on the receipt of your answer of the 29th, to think, in a matter of so great and vital importance to me and my family, that you should so coolly inform me that the trustees have appointed that committee from their own members, and that the meeting should have been appointed in such a place and at such a time. I wish you to say to Dr. Torsey that if he chooses to proceed in this sad and heart-rending case in that manner, self-respect forbids me to take any action before a committee which I have no voice in selecting."

If the object of this investigation was really to bring out all the facts possible in this sad case of the departure and death of Miss Greene, and to ascertain if Dr. T., or any one connected with the care and control of that institution, was in any way to blame, and to satisfy the friends of Miss G., and the public, who, to some extent, to say the least, believe that a great wrong was done by some one, then every possible means should have been taken to give her parents and friends a fair hearing. An entirely disinterested committee should have been selected; a proper time and place should have been agreed upon; all parties should have had ample time to prepare for the hearing. Then the public would have placed confidence in their decision. It would have allayed the excitement.

My objection to the committee was that they all were members of the trustees, directly interested to sustain their teachers and the school. The trustees consist of twenty-six gentlemen, scattered over the State, most of them belonging to the Methodists, and selected as interested persons, who are expected to work for the interest of this school. Two of those trustees belong to, and are the leading spirits of that faculty, namely, H. P. Torsey, and F. A. Robinson, who is a brother to Torsey's wife. The reader will now see how this matter stands. Dr. T. and some of his associates are accused of dealing under prejudice, unjustly and wrongfully, with an old student laboring under public censure. This man (who, by reference to their annual catalogue you will see, stands at the head of the list of Trustees as President) seeks to clear himself. He goes to his friends to their annual State Conference holden at Bath. He there makes a smooth speech, wherein he alludes to this affair. He has well matured what he wished to say, to arouse the whole conference to defend and sustain the reputation of that school. After alluding to attacks which some would make, or had made, of this affair to injure this school, he, in substance, says, speaking to the conference, " This school is your school; its reputation is yours to sustain and defend." Wasn't this well put to the members of that conference, who were to go forth to their respective appointments, and each would be expected to work for this their pet institution? The reputation of their school is at stake, — his reputation is at stake, — and this cunning old fox expects that, through this conference of ministers, the members, on their respective charges, will also labor for the school; and, when they do that, they must also sustain him and his reputation. The public will see whether I am correct or not. Robinson says, at an informal meeting held at Bath a few weeks since, " The committee was indicated." It is fair to suppose that this informal meeting took place soon after this speech of Torsey's; and it is also fair to suppose that he or his special friends managed to get such a committee as he wished selected. As this gentleman, S. R. Bearce, of whom I have before spoken, was one of this committee, I could not expect justice from him, who had given so hasty and decided an opinion in advance of any trial; and, further, as one of the leading members of this committee had already appeared, through a public journal, in a lengthy article in Torsey's defence, and the management of this institution. My objection to the time and place was, that it was on the day of, and one hour after, the anniversary exercises were advertised to commence; when and where it must be all excitement and hurry for the next two days, — when and where the very air is tainted with and every breath is expected to be blown for Torsey and this institution. Some of their friends have given this as a reason or excuse for their neglect to look after and take care of my daughter, because of the approaching anniversary, two weeks ahead, — that the faculty were so much engrossed in preparation for the same. In one year they invite me to an investigation just as the opening exercises commence, when the time of the faculty must be nearly all taken up in the performances. All must see that they, the faculty, meant no such searching investigation as is reported that they had. I must have occupied two days, at least, to have fairly presented my case to the committee. Was this a proper time to investigate the cause of the death of my child? Was this a public or private investigation? By the notice I received I supposed it was to be public. I am informed by one who made numerous inquiries that day, on the Hill, of various students and others, about such a hearing, that he found but one person, and that was a lady student to whom I had written about the meeting, who had any knowledge that such an investigation was to be had; and by the way this man Torsey, — who pretends and testified before this committee how long it was before he knew L. had gone so publicly on the stage as to be seen from the college to get on to it at ten o'clock in the forenoon, in front of his house, and who was so indifferent or undecided as to wait until six o'clock at night before any one started to notify me, — could watch and know that this lady student had received a letter from me, and was so impertinent as to go to this student (who was to graduate the next day, and just then would feel a great hesitancy to deny his request), and ask her for that letter, which he took immediately and read before this committee, as I am informed. It is evident that he did not understand the reason of that letter being sent her at that time. I leave him to enjoy all the credit which he will gain in that transaction. At the special time and place, and when the trustees and committee were assembled, one gentleman present, on motion and by vote, was allowed to remain while the investigation proceeded; the other gentleman was questioned as to who he was, where he belonged, and what his business was there. A motion was made to exclude him; but, before that motion was put, it was suggested that the motion had better not be put, as the gentleman would understand and would withdraw without being voted out. This gentleman then said he understood this to be a public meeting; if so, he should remain; if private, he would withdraw. They said many other things about some other business to be done before they proceeded with the investigation. At the suggestion of the trustees he finally withdrew. Subsequently at about six o'clock at night he was notified that he could attend at that adjourned meeting. Query: Was this a public or private investigation? I will call it *mongrel*. But this gentleman tells me it was certainly intended to be private. With Torsey and his special friends as witnesses, what other result and report could the public expect than what has appeared in some of the public journals? To what extent this has allayed the public feeling, and relieved Torsey and his associates from blame, I am unable to say. To show the unfairness of this transaction, suppose I had selected a committee of my friends, and had appointed some public day for a hearing at my house in Peru, and then, about one week before the hearing, notified Torsey to be present, and make such defence for himself and associates as he chose, in regard to their doings and my daughter leaving the school. How would he and his associates have treated such a proposition? But I am aware that the trustees may say "Mr. Greene was no party to this transaction. We were only investigating the doings of our teachers or faculty at our school. One of our members wrote and invited him to be present, etc. He has no right to complain of our action." If they choose to treat this matter (the cause of the death of my child) in that way, they can do so. I can only say, if this was their case they might look upon such action in a different light; they might think this was treading on delicate ground. You are interested to sustain this school; you were selected as such to work for and to sustain its reputation; and when you attempt to investigate the cause of my child fleeing from your principal, and to an untimely death, you should do it fairly, and not rely upon your own faculty's statement and other interested witnesses to fully justify and exonerate them in this sad case. There is not a member of this faculty or trustees, or an intelligent person in any community, who would refer the smallest matter in dispute to such interested referees. There is not a lawyer to be found so void of fairness as to advise a client to attempt or accept such a proposition. It seems to me that Dr. Torsey's course, in this attempt to clear himself, in so unfair and unjustifiable a manner, in so grave and wretched an affair, is enough to convince the public that he wofully wronged, and wickedly neglected to care for our child. If it was not so he would not have made such desperate efforts to clear himself from public censure. Was there anything done to save her? Oh! her bitter words in her letter : " If I could have had an opportunity on the Hill to retrieve the past ! If this thing had not been made common talk and public property, there might have been a future for me." These words ought to wring in Torsey's ears while he lives. He made this appear so to her. He says he told her the school knew it; and his urging her to go home in disgrace, to leave that day, — this, no doubt, is what she means by not having an opportunity on the Hill to retrieve the past. Again she writes: "They tried to make me account for all the little things lost during the term." When they, as Miss Case said they did, searched that little fancy trunk, holding about a quart, were they looking for articles of clothing in that? Were they not trying to make her account for all the lost articles lost that term? and, were they not disgracing, abusing, and driving her to distraction, when they, as Mrs. Daggett told me, examined her person, and the under-clothes she had on, so far as to see that her chemise was marked with her own name? Mr. Daggett admitted to me that, when he was called in to assist his wife and Miss Case in this examination (as I suppose after they had exhausted their skill and abuse on my poor girl), he questioned her about two linen handkerchiefs ; he would not say that he was cross and severe on her ; but I have very good reasons to believe that he was severe beyond reason. In his testimony before the committee of trustees he would not say that he was not cross with her. Have they found those small articles which they wrongfully accused L. of taking, but did not find, after pursuing her and her sister to the shameful extent to which they did? Why do Torsey and Robinson continue to harp about that skeleton key? They told us in that faculty meeting that they did not accuse her of using it wrongfully. She, in her class letter, says: "My having that key did look bad; but I do not believe that they really thought I used it wrongfully. I certainly never did." When I called on Daggett to see that skeleton key, he and his wife said they never saw or knew anything about the key until L. left. The faculty said they said nothing personally to her about the key, but had told students, publicly, that if any of them should have in their possession such keys, and things should be lost, they would be suspected. Why lecture students publicly, if the having a skeleton key was an unheard-of event, and the keeping of one such a crime as to cause them to write continually about it to enlarge her crime? They well knew it is no uncommon thing in this and other schools for students to have such keys. An old student at this school told me they should not have thought it any harm to have kept one as a curiosity; and yet, L. having one in her possession. (although given to her by one of their own students, of which Mrs. Daggett gave me the name of the giver) is spread abroad by Torsey and Robinson, both private and public, as a heinous offence, — a crime. They not only tried to impress upon her, this poor distracted girl, "the enormity of her crime" (Miss Case's own language), but they try to "impress" the public with the same. That key I have never been able to find.

In that faculty meeting, one week after L. had left, and our fears were that she was dead, he (Torsey) seemed desirous to know what we were going to say about the matter, — thought it best for us to say but little in regard to the same. Yes; this unfeeling man thought we could lose our child in such a heart-rending manner and say but little about it, while he and his associates send broadcast over the State all kinds of stories. We must believe all they say, take all his insulting letters, let them connive to get up student committee's reports and trustee committee's reports, publish and send them over the State, and her friends not say a word. Does it look as Robinson writes, "after as private an examination as possible," when Chestina and Mr. Chandler, who came home with her, knew all; Mr. Swagler tells L. the morning she left he knew all; Miss Case takes all her class, before L. left that morning, and tells them all; Torsey tells her that morning the school know it? Is it true that they kept it as private as possible, or was it not making it public? I never accused him of publicly reprimanding her before the school. This sly, cunning man has a different way, I think, to accomplish his ends. But his often and repeated denial of doing so has of late led me to think that something of that kind was done by him. I submit to the public if I have not shown him to have been her enemy for a long time. At any rate, she looked upon him as such, and a revengeful one, too. Does not this pursuing their dead student, to disgrace her memory and to injure her friends, show that Louise well understood that man? Did she not understand his power and will to do, to accomplish his object? If any one doubts his infallibility, then private and public indignation must be aroused against them. They are not content with the death of their pupil, who made immediate, full, frank confession and restitution, and atoned with her life for that small offence; but even now it comes to me that they threaten, if I dare defend my child's character from numerous misrepresentations set afloat, that they will further disgrace her memory and injure her friends. Therefore we or the public *need* not be surprised at any stories, or any means they may take to accomplish that end. · In the language of their circulars, can "Parents feel assured that their sons and daughters will find here a *safe* and pleasant home"?

Sarah Dow, one of L.'s class, tells me lately that Miss Case, the preceptress, on the morning of May 23, before Louise left, called all the class into her room in the college, and told them all about the affair, and said she could tell them now; she had not had liberty to do so before. Then somebody must have given her liberty to publish all to her class. Who but the faculty could do so, of which Torsey is chief? This must be about the time T. was talking with L., and telling her the school knew it. Did Miss Case know that she would be expelled? It does look like that; or she would not have been telling all to them unless she was preparing them for that event, reporting all in such a manner as to make it look, as Miss Fuller expressed it, " so large then to us."

It is clear to my mind that this one of the leading spirits of the faculty then knew as well as Torsey that she would be expelled. The reader will see that, any way which they can explain it, they did not mean to spare her feelings or save her from disgrace. My poor girl knew it well. One other member of her class writes me, June, 1867, that Miss Case did, on that fatal morning, "immediately after breakfast, call our class into her room" (the quick eye of our poor girl no doubt saw this movement, and quickly divined her intention);" and the principal object, she said, that she had, in calling us into her room, was to tell us her course in regard to the matter from the beginning, and also to tell that L. confessed to the charges brought against her." Then her first object was to explain and clear herself. (The others were also very ready to do that.) The next object was to publish her private confession to all the class. Why, in the name of all that is good and noble, did not this preceptress, who should have acted the motherly, or at least a friendly, part, and extend her protecting care over all she in part presides over, those whom she is directing and controlling, — why, instead of making all so public and to explain her course to others, did she not, the evening before, go to my lone, distressed, and distracted child, and speak words of encouragement and comfort to her troubled mind, and give her kindly advice, to see if she did not want some assistance?

Benjamin Harriman told me, at his house on Kent's Hill, May 26, three days after L. had gone, that just before he started for the depot with his coach, on which she rode away, he heard something of her trouble, and knew by her looks that she was feeling bad, although she tried to keep up favorable appearances, and saw she was clad in old apparel, and that she was taking nothing with her but a little reticule. His fears were excited for her safety, and while disposing, at the depot, of the baggage and express matter, he thought he ought to get on to the train and go to see what became of her, but could not think of any one to take charge of his stage team. He thought he would gain time, and, if possible, before the train started, go and talk with her. Just as he got through, he started to go to her on the platform. As soon as she saw him coming towards her, she turned and went directly into the cars, and, as they were about to start, he did not pursue. He then learned that she had purchased a ticket for Lewiston; and, on his return to the Hill, meeting Miss Reed on the street, she says, on speaking of her sudden departure without taking her baggage, and in her ordinary clothing, and fearing the sad result liable to follow, he was affected to tears,—he saying, at her request, that he would take a team and go with Chestina to Lewiston, in pursuit of Louise. If this arrangement or request of Miss Reed had immediately been put into execution (and I have no doubt but what it would have been had Dr. Torsey been out of the way, where he could not have been consulted), she doubtless would have been saved, as about three hours would have taken them to Lewiston, where Louise remained more than four hours at the Elm House after a team could have been started by Mr. Harriman to pursue her. There can be but little doubt but Torsey's influence prevented Miss Reed's attempt to get a team started to pursue her. Miss Reed says, after the long and wretched delay, in which she and Chestina got all out of patience, heart-sick, in waiting until six o'clock at night, when the team came to take Chestina home, she felt as if it was too late to save her; that before that team could reach me and I could get to Lewiston, she would get beyond our reach, or, what she more feared, would be dead.

An old student informs us at our home that Louise was once, in his and in the presence of the assembled school, at prayers, severely reprimanded by one of the faculty, because she did not *rise* during singing; and after she had given as a reason for not rising that she was sick and unable to stand up, he, with harsh and ungentlemanly language, calling her by name, sent her to her room. Louise had told her mother of the same, and said she felt so sick during prayers that she could not stand. This was some time during the last year of her stay at that school. Dr. Torsey, at one time after prayers, while lecturing the students, and in a slurring manner, called her by name in regard to some small matter about leave of absence, all tending to show their prejudice and desire to wound her feelings. The student above referred to told us of a case which, to his mind, was clear, where

Torsey, on account of the religious sentiments or opinions of a student, — an able writer, one who was excluded from, and was not allowed a chance to compete for, distinction in composition, on account of his well-known religious opinions, which came in contact with the established religion of this school, — a great outburst of indignation was expressed against an argument which this student made in their lyceum, on the affirmative of the question, "Whatever is, is right." He was talked to and his arguments ridiculed. Ever after he was not allowed a fair chance as a writer or debater in the school.

Another student writes me, and among other things, speaking of Torsey, says : "In fact, I do not admire his religious belief, neither do I admire the gentleman, not because of any particular individual misusage, but simply did not like his way of acting towards those who did not believe as he would choose to have them. I noticed it on several occasions, and others with me in that manner of thinking. It is my private opinion that he has his favorites, and that those favorites are favored, though in a sly way."

Dr. Torsey is only a man possessed of human nature, and is as liable, when in a strait place, to dissemble and deny what he did do, as others have done to screen themselves from blame. If a guilty person says he is innocent, will that answer if all the circumstances point the other way? If a man threatens to burn your buildings, and he is proved to have been out and near your place the night they are burned, with materials to fire them, his denial will not clear him from suspicion. If you are aroused in the night by some one who has stealthily entered your house, you make a vigorous and successful spring at and finally overpower him; and if he sould say he was tired, cold, and came in to get lodging for the night, would you believe him, if he was armed with a revolver, dirk, and other deadly weapons? Judge and jury would infer his motives, — he would be held as a burglar.

I find, on the 23d of May, 1866 (after my daughter had for the past thirty-six or forty hours been implicated, harassed, and pursued by those under Dr. T.'s control and direction); Dr. Torsey taking her alone in a room in the college, and having a long conversation with her; and, on his leaving her, I find her without saying a word to any other person in that building, immediately taking off her gold sleeve-buttons, her class ring, breaking from her neck a small cord on which she had long worn that very little key which opened that fancy trunk, and evidently, at this time, hastily writing those words on the lap of an envelope, "Heart breaking; dearly beloved, adieu," and tucking them into her diary, which she left in her trunk. I find her going to her sister's room, in another house, in an excited state of mind. Failing to see her, she writes a short note, telling her she was going to Lewiston, etc. I find her leaving money in her trunk, and going in her poorest apparel, taking nothing of importance with her. I find her taking the stage in front of Torsey's house, at ten in the forenoon. I find him in his stable, which is attached to his house. Before twelve he is notified just how she left, and the great fear of her destruction made known to him. I find him parleying, delaying, consuming time, — saying he could or would do this, that, or the other thing, but doing nothing to recover her for eight long hours after her departure. I find him telling her sister it would not have been best for her to have gone on to the stage, etc., and telling Miss Reed that L. said she wanted it kept from the school, — she stay and graduate, — and that she told him if she could not graduate, there was no future for her; thus plainly indicating to him her awful fate. I find him writing me various things about her leaving, telling us things inconsistent with what he has written, and withholding things from us, which he had told others, about her leaving. I find her writing her sister the day she left, that Dr. T. advised her to leave that day. I find him long before telling her she could not expect any more favors of him or of the school; and if she should do anything that looked like a wilful violation of any rule, she could expect but little forbearance from the teachers. I find she had confessed, privately, to three of them, just what and all she had done, and the reason why she had done so, excepting the money, — she gave no reason for that. I find her writing that she felt herself guilty of but one crime, — the taking of the money, — and saying that was a mystery to her. At length her wasted form is discovered. With all this, and many other petty annoyances, with his well-known prejudice, I have a right to doubt his, and the other inconsistent statements coming from that faculty. I, and the public, have a right to infer and judge, under all the circumstances of this sad case, what was most likely said and done which sent her to an untimely death. And when I find him writing me, May 27, 1866, four days after she left. "I had a long conversation with her the morning she left, and urged upon her two things." After stating the first, he says, — second, "that she go at once to her father and mother." Does that look like allowing her to graduate, within twelve days, when he was urging her to go at once home to her parents, in disgrace? Who will say he expected her to return and graduate? And when he writes me, June 30, 1866, "She was not sent home," — he saw that was too bare faced a lie, and he erased the words "sent home," and wrote the word "expelled" over them, making the sentence read, — "She was not expelled." Judge ye. whether this statement is true! I cannot see it in that light, when she writes that he said, "We won't call it expulsion, but I advise you to go home to-day." What in the name of Heaven was he doing but expelling her? God being my judge, I believe he is attempting to palm off upon me an absolute falsehood. And can he make the public believe that he was honest when he told Chestina and Miss Reed that he had no fears of her destruction? Is he more dull of apprehension than many students who greatly feared for her fate as soon as they knew how she had gone? He who knew her best, her sensitive nature, knew all about how she had gone, has no fears, tells about her going into a factory or running away. O consistency! He is a sharp, shrewd man, and thinks he can readily read characters, discern motives, and quickly anticipate results. Don't tell me he did or could not understand what would most likely be the result. Under all the circumstances and evidences, I have come to the following conclusion, and from which I cannot retract, unless some new evidence shall be disclosed: — That as he (Torsey) found that he could not control and mould her opinions, and as she would not consent to his infallibility, he became prejudiced against her, — her influence, religiously, did not suit him, she not being with them heart and soul (as he expressed it), — this annoyed and perplexed him much; and now, when he found she was in trouble, he thinks, I now have a good opportunity, Miss Greene, I will make you feel my power. I will so manage as to make you see that you have no chance to graduate, without saying so in so many words. (I do not believe he ever told any student so; he has a different way of accomplishing his purpose.) I will, when I get you to see the hopelessness of your case, advise you to leave. Before your parents know anything about your trouble, you will be far away, as they may make trouble. This will disgrace you, and will also punish your father for his plain and pertinent letter to me two years ago. You will live through it, I think, — he not caring or thinking but little what would become of her. After she had gone, and when he found just how, and all about her leaving, he, at a glance, saw the serious turn the case was taking, and the result that would be likely to follow; he was greatly perplexed to know how to manage, or what to say or do. Hence his pretence that he did not know she was gone for some time. Then he hesitates, argues, delays, goes away; comes again, and tells what he had arranged to do; and then there is another two or three hours' delay before he puts that arrangement into execution. He saw the fix he would be in if Harriman and Chestina had immediately pursued and been successful in securing her return, or saving her life. She would have confronted him before her friends, and said,

"You sent me away in disgrace, and why do you pursue me?" This meeting her and her friends he wished to avoid. Hence his neglect to pursue her, and his long delay to notify me, so as to give her time to escape beyond the reach of friends, or that the result might be as it was, before any one could reach her and save her life.

If her crime had been a hundred-fold greater, so much greater the necessity and the responsibility resting upon him. He discloses to *us* his wicked deception *most* when he tries to make students and others believe he loved her, was tender of her feelings, and felt bad about her misfortune and death, when everything showed to the contrary. This outward appearance he attempts for effect. So is his great effort to be particularly kind to the students since this awful tragedy. He knows his reputation is at stake, and he needs all the friends which he can make; and I have no doubt but what many have been the favors that students have received on account of the suffering and death of our poor girl. This man has been at the head of that school so long that in my opinion he has become arbitrary and overbearing. Authority and power for a long time makes men so. If he is that good and noble man, that kind and Christ-like Christian, some would have the public believe, why does he pursue this vindictive course towards her parents; why write me his insulting letters? It cannot be anything that I have written him, for the reader has seen every word I have written him since L. left, in those two letters before given. Parents who shall read this, were it your child, should you be willing to bear all we have and not say a word? No, you would not only say, but you would have all you could do to keep your hands off of him. It may be with all those who dealt so summarily with L. on the Hill, that their character from childhood up could stand such an ordeal as they are applying to hers, and each and all come out unscathed; it may be so, with that committee of students, and with Dr. Torsey; but a close examination might disclose the fact that all have not escaped having some unfavorable reports circulated about them, at some period of their lives.

One of my neighbors (kindly, he may have thought) advised me not to come out and make any defence for my child; said that a Methodist minister told his wife that they at Kent's Hill had fifteen counts against her, — fifteen thefts as he took it to be; and I have no doubt but thousands are made to believe such stories. If that be true then I have over sixty just such counts against them, besides the cash, post-office stamps, clothing, and various other articles lost there during the five years and previous to those lost the last term.

I sought through the press to give our child in death the benefit of her previous good character, by publishing those numerous certificates, and strong proofs of her ever good standing and moral worth from a child up to this sad affair, not saying a word about or blaming any one in regard to her leaving and subsequent death. A large portion of the press (as I believe for fear of losing the patronage of this Kent's Hill influence and that denomination) refused to publish those statements or certificates of her previous good moral character. The publication of those certificates in some of the papers seemed to stir up this faculty and their friends everywhere to fresh attacks on her character; they seem to act as if they thought their only chance to escape public censure was to stigmatize her previous character, enlarge upon her last act, and make her crime appear so large that they would be justified in their treatment to her, and they take shelter under their cry of "Thief, thief." The refusal of so large a portion of the press to publish those certificates, and the publishing of the other side by some of the papers, leaves me no alternative but to seek some other source to reach the public, and vindicate her previous character, and to show the great wrongs done her while living, and since she fled from that institution.

The friends of Dr. T. may say as did the friends of Prof. Webster of Boston, in the Parkman murder case,—"Oh! he is so nice a man; his reputation stands so high; he is clear; he never did that act. He says he did not, and denies all knowledge of the crime,—the whole affair; and you ought to believe him. Why, Prof. Webster has not murdered, has not cut up, boiled, or burnt his victim's remains. That is horrible! too bad to think of in this Christian land." And people would look at each other with astonishment when some expressed their belief that it was true. Yet it was so. And this grave professor denied and lied at every turn in his case until he found he must swing for it. Then, he owned and confessed all. And so it has been in a thousand cases. None can tell what man possessed of human nature will do under bad circumstances.

The reader can never realize how grateful we feel towards those of her class who asked Miss Reed to go to Torsey and see what could be done; and to Miss Reed, for her efforts and earnest desire to get Harriman and Chestina started immediately after her. And our *abhorrence* and *contempt* for this modern *Nero*, who could fiddle, play upon words to consume time, prevent pursuit, while our poor child, heart-broken, was fleeing from him (who then stood in the place of, and should have extended parental protection to her), from all that was dear to her on earth, and going to destruction.

I can now, as it were, hear the moans, the sobs, coming up from that lonely forest, where our darling child so terribly perished. Her dying wail, saying to that heartless man, "You saw me in great distress and you ministered not unto me; you saw me in trouble, and you took me not in; you knew of my terrible disappointment, my heart-rending feelings, — for I told you I could not go home to my parents in disgrace. I told you if I could not graduate, there was no future for me. You advised me to leave. You sent me heart-broken to an untimely death, when you could have saved me. When you come up to the judgment-seat, where you and I shall stand around that great white throne, and before Him who knows all things, will you then and there attempt to excuse yourself to the Judge of all, as you did to my parents, and say, 'Your daughter was of age, and I had no right to control her; she was under censure, and it would be unproper to have sent her to my house and to my wife'?" Torsey and her other accusers on the Hill may have religion, but, I pray God to give me a different kind of religion, — a religion which shows some of the precept and examples taught by Christ while upon earth.

In laying before my readers some of our departed child's writing, permit me to state, that the first piece given was written by her when less than ten years old, the first she ever wrote, and then will follow others written all the way along from ten to sixteen, before she went to Kent's Hill, with some written after and while she was attending there; but as a large portion of her writings are lost there with her other things, we cannot give some of her ablest productions to the public, unless they shall be restored to us.

LIBERTY.

Everything that God has made loves liberty. The little birds that sing so merrily to us, when deprived of liberty, lose their cheerfulness, and often pine away and die. The lambs that sport so gayly in the green fields, when confined, bleat piteously and seem to say, let me go; and even the little worm that crawls beneath our feet, when confined to a narrow space, shows discontent. If liberty then be so dear to the animal creation, how much more so must it be to God's intelligent beings! And how great must be the sin of those who deprive their fellow-beings of that liberty they so highly prize themselves, and also take away the key of knowledge that they may better subject them to bondage!

HOW WE SPENT INDEPENDENCE DAY, 1857.

Every one said Independence day would be pleasant; and so it was. Every one intended to enjoy themselves to the best of their ability, myself among the number. A thousand schemes for pleasure were proposed, and finally it was unanimously agreed that a visit to Rumford Falls would be just the thing, away from the bustle and confusion attendant upon a crowded celebration, away from the crowded street and the vulgarity and drunkenness that usually characterize such a miscellaneous gathering, to that scene of rural beauty. Accordingly six o'clock A.M. found us on our way to that delightful place, in company with a few of our intimate friends and school-mates. The day was warm and pleasant; the tall trees waved their leafy branches above our heads; the tiny birds warbled their morning songs, and all nature seemed to participate in our enjoyment. After riding about eight miles, a loud rumbling sound gave notice of our approach to the cataract. Leaving our teams a short distance, we walked up to the very brink of the precipice which overhung the water, when a magnificent sight lay beneath our feet. The verdant hue of the overhanging trees blended with the deep blue waters as they foamed and dashed down their rocky bed; the everlasting mountains that proudly rear their lofty heads in the distance; the clear blue sky over our heads; and the fancifully woven carpet of green grass spread out beneath our feet,—all these and many other attractions formed a picture worthy of a painter's skill. Beneath the wide-spreading branches of a noble tree, where a spring of clear cold water bubbled up from the rock below to quench our thirst, we seated ourselves to rest, and also to partake of the various refreshments provided for us.

After enjoying a quiet chat and a good lunch, we took a last look of that charming spot, and soon were rapidly travelling on the homeward way, stopping, however, a short time at the house of one of our number, where we were entertained with a feast of good things. The old family clock struck six as we arrived home again, and methinks in the future, when we look back upon the days that are past and gone, our minds will delight to linger upon the remembrance of that happy Independence day.

LIFE: WHAT IS IT?

What is life? — to some, "a breath,
A vapor flying to the skies;"
To others, a gay, fantastic path
Bestrown with flowery phantasies.

What is life? — a dream to those
Who idly stray until its end;
A dream, upon whose final close
A sad awakening shall attend.

What is life? — a journey long
  And drear, when travelled all alone,
But when companions cheer the way,
  One upon which we long would stay.

What is life? — a darksome night,
  With but one star to light the gloom,
And on Death's wing we take our flight,
  To dwell 'neath Heaven's unclouded sun.

Peru, Dec. 24, 1859.

THOUGHTS BY THE WAYSIDE.

"O Mr. B., it seems too bad to cut down that clover," said I to our hired man, one sultry summer day, as he was busily engaged in mowing down the fragrant clover that lifted its tall heads, crowned with beautiful blossoms in our little enclosure. "Why?" queried he. "Because it smells so sweetly and looks so pretty." "Its beauty will soon fade," he replied, resuming his labor.

I, too, turned again to my work, but his thoughtless words had awakened a train of thought in my mind; and in fancy I again beheld the countenance of a lovely maiden with whom I associated in my early school-days, and whose history I well knew. Hers was a beauty of the regal cast: wavy hair of purplish blackness, flashing black eyes, a form of stately beauty, and fair, round face, every feature of which was cast in beauty's mould. An enviable lot was hers; the only daughter of an aristocratic family, her wish was law; her pleasure, their chief aim to secure. Petted and indulged by her parents, flattered by her associates, to her life must have worn a cheerful look, and earth a paradise.

But soon the scene changed. Pecuniary embarrassments swept away her father's fortune, and with it went most of their fashionable friends. Death came and removed one after another of that family band, till parents, brothers, all were gone. She was almost penniless and alone in a great city. Alas! too truly had she learned the mutability of earthly enjoyments; and, as I recalled the story of her misfortunes, I thought of the farmer's words, "It will soon fade." Gone were her wealth and her numerous friends and relatives, — her earthly all, faded and withered beneath the sharp scythe of time.

Again, I see a young man, his cheeks flushed with ambition of youth, and eyes sparkling at the thought of the future glory that should be his; of the wealth he would gain and the fame that should surround his name with a halo of glory. Again I saw him in riper manhood; he had gained that emolument for which he toiled. Wealth had come at his call, yet it brought increased cares. Ambition had raised him to an equality with great men of his age; but it brought no real happiness. He was blessed with a model wife and family to sympathize with him in affliction and to rejoice at his joy; yet mingled with pure affection was much dross. He had reached the summit of the hill, and now enjoyed the world's favor; yet one thing was wanting; without it, true happiness cannot exist. He had sought it in pleasure, but it was not there; in riches, but found it not; in fame, but the search proved useless; in the busy walks of fashion he found it not; neither did it dwell in the halls of literature and art. Despairingly he turned away, thinking that true happiness dwelt not on earth, when his eyes rested on a humble volume lying on the shelves of his bookcase. It was old and faded, and bore marks of neglect by the dust which had gathered thickly upon its lids. Thinking to beguile a few moments, he listlessly opened the book, and the first passage which met his eye read thus: "Come unto me, all ye that are weary and heavy laden, and I will give you rest." Rest! was not this the treasure for which he had searched long and diligently, but found it not? Rest for the weary and heavy laden; was he not wearied with toil and cares?—heavy laden with burdens of anxiety? Instantly he resolved to seek that rest, to obtain that peace in the way which the Bible pointed out. He was this time successful in his search. By slow but sure degrees his mind began to comprehend the *true* end of life,—to see that not man's but God's favor must be sought, ere the longings of his immortal spirit could be satisfied. And when this was done, when the barriers of pride and sin were removed, and the light of religion shone upon his soul, his cup of happiness was full to overflowing. Did our Saviour call home his darling child? He could look with an eye of faith up to that blessed land where sorrow and suffering come no more, and behold his child among the angel band which dwells at the right hand of our Father, and rejoicing in his smiles. Did men scorn and despise him? Turning to God's holy word, he reads, "Blessed are ye, when men shall revile and persecute you." And when the death-angel came knocking at the door of his soul, he could say, with the inspired prophet, "Though I walk through the valley of the shadow of death, I will fear no evil, for Thy rod and Thy staff will comfort and sustain me." Such piety, like fruitful seed planted in fertile soil, grows and expands, choking out each obnoxious weed, till, transplanted, it blooms forever in more congenial climes.

Sorrow and disappointments may overwhelm us; friends may depart and enemies exult in our distress; every earthly pleasure may wither and fade, as the morning dewdrop from the grass, or as the grass itself sinks beneath the sharp scythe of the mower; yet with religion for our support, we shall safely tread the mazy labyrinth of life, and finally repose in that land of the blest, where sickness shall come no more, and where enjoyments are eternal and unfading.

LINES.

I sat within my chamber,
   One cold and wintry night;
Around me winds were blowing,
   And the moon refused her light.

And as I sat there thinking
   Of the love that once was mine,
Of the friend, who, in life's morning,
   Was cut down, by the hand of Time,—

My mourning heart cried wildly,
   "How can I walk alone
The dark and dreary pathway
   That leads to our Father's home?

"I miss thy bright, sweet presence,
   O friend forever gone!
While *others* walk in gladness,
   Must I wander alone?

"Even *now* my feet are weary,
   And hardly find the track;
If thou, love, could'st but guide me,
   I'd fear no turning back."

The darkness grew still deeper,
   Still wilder came my cry,—
"I *cannot* live without thee;
   O Father, let me die!"

When on my spirit vision
   Two forms were shadowed forth,
One, with a crown of glory,
   And one like those of earth.

"Fear not, for I am with you,"
   Said Jesus, from on high;
And the voice of my lost darling
   Whispered, "I, too, am nigh."

IN MEMORY OF A MUCH LOVED FRIEND.

Hard, indeed, it was to leave thee,
   Beautiful, in life's bright bloom:
Harder *still* it was to lay thee
   In the cold and silent tomb.

Yet we know our God is righteous,
  In his presence thou art blest;
And we, praying, hope to greet thee,
  In that sweet and sinless rest.

Will heaven's sweet and thrilling music
  Fill thy heart with sweet refrain?
'Midst the joys of angel worship
  Wilt one thought of me retain?

Will affection's strong, deep tendrils,
  Severed here by death's rude hand,—
Will they not be reaching downwards,
  Yearning for me in that land?

Father, grant me faith and patience,
  Strength to wait, and labor on;
That in death I may be worthy
  To arise, and join mine own.

SPRING.

Night is gathering round us, twilight veils the sky;
Whispering winds are telling spring is drawing nigh.
Birds are flying northward, in angelic notes
Music sweet is swelling from their little throats;

Calling to each other in the early morn,
Waking us poor mortals ere 'tis fairly dawn;
Graceful little creatures, fairy-like and gay,
Harbingers of summer, everywhere are they.

From the earth uprising, robed in brightest green,
Clothing earth in beauty, the springing grass is seen;
Trees once bare and ragged, angular and slim,
Beneath spring's genial influence, soon will look quite trim.

Cedar, spruce, and hemlock, soon you'll charm no more,
Budding oak and maple will eclipse you soon;
All nature stirring round us, all earth with life replete,
Proclaims that earth is waking from her long winter's sleep.

These are but a small portion of her early writings. I would have been glad to have given the public the story written by her at the age of twelve years, but the length of the same, prevents it. I give these as samples to show the drift of her youthful mind. The next is an account of her first start for Kent's Hill, in 1861, the day she left home.

A LEAF FROM MY JOURNAL.

Tuesday, March 12, 1861.— This morning we left our pleasant home for a sojourn among strangers. The sky was clear and bright, and gave promise of a pleasant day, and the air was just sharp enough to send the blood dancing through every vein, giving clearness and vigor to both body and mind. Leaving home is usually an unpleasant affair to us, but we had looked forward so long and so eagerly to this journey that its approach was a signal for rejoicing. What if we *were* going among entire strangers? we should soon get acquainted; if we did not, 'twas no matter. We knew we should like, and started in the best of spirits.

A journey of so much importance must have some remarkable incidents. Ours first happened in this way. On our way to R. it became necessary to cross the Androscoggin river on the ice, which was rather a hazardous proceeding. We got along well enough, however, till we reached the farther shore, when crash! splash! and the first thing I knew I found myself sitting in not the most graceful attitude in a snow-bank : my companion near by was oh-ing and oh-ing at a great rate, while the big trunk stood on end between us. Afar off was seen Charley-horse, walking demurely along just as if nothing at all had happened, and no doubt pleased at finding his load so suddenly lightened. At first I could hardly tell how I came there, but on looking towards the river I saw at once that near the shore the ice had suddenly given away, causing the sleigh to plunge down two or three feet, and necessarily throwing us out. Luckily the shore was so near that we landed on the bank instead of going into the river, for a cold water plunge-bath would not have been, just at that time, very agreeable. We gatherep up ourselves and accoutrements, and finding nothing damaged (except the *ice*, which was badly fractured), went on our way rejoicing. (My " Leaf" being covered, I must finish my story another time.)

THE ANGEL'S CHOICE.

When the day was finished, and the starlight
   Had fallen soft over the earth,
From out the beautiful cloud-land
   The angels were gazing forth.

Long they gazed, for our earth was lovely,
   With no trace of sorrow or sin;
Like the radiant bowers of Eden
   Ere the serpent had entered in.

But list! for the silence is broken,
   And forth, with a tiny footful,
Steps one from the band of seraphs,
   And soft to the others she calls: —

"Sisters! of all the bright things
   That unto mankind are given,

  Which would you choose to dwell in,
   If earth was your home, and not heaven ? "

" In a cascade bright and sparkling,"
 Said one of the laughing elves;
" Or, down 'mid the coral islands,
 Where the giant sea-monsters dwell."

" In a rose, that all might love me;
 In a diamond, that I might endure;"
But the first angel spoke up quickly,—
 " In a snow-flake, that I might be pure!"

CHANGE.

The sunshine would not seem so bright,
 If there were never storms;
We greet the spring with deep delight,
 We hail the harvest morns.

We smile to see the busy bee
 Sip summer's golden grains,
Yet turn well pleased to home of ease
 When white-robed winter reigns.

The sweet would never seem so sweet
 If it could always last,
And "written language" fail complete,
 If "spoken" words were past.

We love our books, yet turn to look
 On nature's wide-spread range;
For mind and matter too, you'll find,
 Seeks everywhere for change.

The past is pleasing in our eyes,
 The present very good;
Yet no man lives who would not grasp
 His future if he could.

GONE HOME.

 With a feeling akin to gladness we utter these words, as one after another of our number goes at the call of duty, or of pleasure, back to the dear home-circle, to mother's love and friends. But when God calls them up yonder, where the home eternal is, the shadow of the golden gates through which they entered rest darkly on our hearts.

 In this room, where his voice was so often heard, it is well for us now to make mention of one who on earth is no more. Will Jones, — he has been with us at many a May walk, and many a festive scene; he has toiled beside us up the rugged hill of science, and made the ascent less wearisome to many a tired traveller.

Would he linger then, when motherland called for her loyal sons? They who knew him best were least surprised when he came to the Hill, a soldier, to bid it a final *good-by*. For by one of those strange foreshadowings of the future, known only to genius-lighted minds, our friend was satisfied that he would never return. But he had heard the voice of duty, and duty to him was law. On Monday, the 1st of February, the 7th Maine Battery left Augusta for Washington; on Friday, the 5th, it was stationed at Camp Berry, East Capitol Hill. Then the fever fell upon him and he saw the familiar faces of far-off friends in Maine; on Kent's Hill he walked again "in the old way," and the " prayers of our chapel" were ringing in his ears. On Monday, March 28th, the news of his sickness first reached us and the next Friday he died. Not died, —

> "There is no death; what seems so is transition.
> This life of mortal breath
> Is but an entrance to the life Elysian
> Whose portals we call death."

Believing this, we may not mourn that only twenty-two short years of earth-life were given to our friend. The school, the great world he would have benefited, the little circle of intimate friends, — a school before unbroken, — may lament their own loss, — his gain. God fitted him for this life, then gave him life eternal.

> "O earth, so full of dreary noises!
> O men, with wailing in your voices!
> O shining gold, the wailer's heap!
> O strife! O curse! that o'er it fall,
> God makes a silence through you all,
> And giveth his beloved sleep."

Spring of 1864.

CONSISTENCY.

Yes, my friends, believe in youthful enthusiasm; like to have young folks lively; tell them to move quick; be cheerful, and at the same time inform your nephew he's going to ruin because he whistles Yankee Doodle, or claps his hand enthusiastically over the speech of Mr. So-and-So.

Cry out against despotism and tyranny; have a mortal horror of the Pope of Rome; hate Catholics, because they are obliged to yield implicit obedience; cause the eyes of little children to dilate with wonder at your marvellous stories of Blue-Beard, who didn't torment his friends while living, — but kindly ate them up; but take care to terrify everybody within the reach of your influence by a series of diminutive despotisms, or irritate them by petty exhibitions of authority.

Make minds your study, that you may do them good (of course), and when you have found their most sensitive spot grasp it with iron fingers. Make jokes; make a thousand of them, and laugh complacently all the while.

Tell your friends it's a fine thing to laugh and be merry; but if a poor, innocent little joke comes unexpected into your presence, annihilate it with a tremendous frown. All this you may do, and more; but remember

"Precept whispers, while example thunders."

ANNIVERSARY DAYS.

And by this term we do not mean those dry intellectual feasts with which college students are supposed to delight their patrons, — such as come to us on the Hill when June comes, let who will be president. But we each set apart a few days from life's common routine, and devote them to the past. Anniversary days! Individuals have them; the nation has them; and once in a great while God puts a distinguishing mark on some part of his time, and it becomes henceforth an anniversary day for all mankind.

We make our anniversaries of vastly different stuff. Some are fine and silken and full of golden gleaming lustre, and when, as time comes round, we bring forth the beautiful garment, it clothes us with joy unspeakable. Then time weaves a gay, flashing garment and we think it will last us forever. But we hang it in memory's closet, and, lo! all its beauty is gone. There is sombre black in that closet, and we wear it at times next our heart.

It is wonderful to think how thickly sown are the seed of these *memory* days. May 27th is an anniversary to some, and yesterday afternoon was to how many?

Birthdays are universal anniversaries; not only our own, but our friends. They have been aptly called mile-stones marking our progress on life's journey, — a journey where all the travellers are homeward bound.

And when the eternal gates are opened to those left behind, there remains only this record, "Died."

"And ever in our hearts we keep
The birthdays of the dead."

The war has made many anniversaries that all coming time will observe. July 4th and Washington's birthday seemed about all the nation used to have in common; but now we must add April 15th and the date of the close of the war.

Grief here and gladness there formed a bond uniting us all. From the beginning God saw the need of these great bonds of a common humanity, and so made the Christian Sabbath consecrated to holy memories of his working and his rest and gave us Christmas week, — an anniversary set apart forever as a memorial of what Christ hath done for all mankind.

LILLA LUNT.

Died of Diphtheria in the Summer of 1862.

Two little hands that at morning
  Were first to be clasped in my own,
And two cunning eyes that, from dawning
  Of day till the starlight and moon
Lit the heavens, never wearied or slumbered,
  And whose glances were like to the gleam
Of the daisies that blossomed in spring-time,
  Near our home on the banks of the stream; —

Fair baby hands whose close clinging
  We almost can feel now at even;
And a voice whose last earth-singing
  Was of mother, home, love, and heaven;
Face whose innocent sweetness
  Never was clouded by care,
Shrouded about and shaded
  By the softest and brownest of hair; —

Little thought we that our darling
  Would be borne from our arms so soon;
Little thought we that spring roses
  Would lie on her breast in the tomb!
Ah well! we must strive to be patient,
  Kneel humbly and bow 'neath the rod;
For we know that our Lily, transplanted,
  Now blooms in the garden of God.

WOMAN'S DUTY AT THE PRESENT TIME

Tread softly, students, in these halls! O man of business, pause,
For a nation bows in sadness now o'er liberty's dear cause.
The downtrod million of the earth have, trembling, staked their all;
With our success their freedom's won, and with us, too, they fal.

While the tramp of gathering thousands is resounding through the land
And brother meeteth brother in death-conflict hand to hand,
Have we no duty to perform, — no laurel crown to win?
Shall woman stand with folded hands before this monster sin?

You've read in history's pages how, when Freedom's Sky grew dark,
'Twas lighted up by woman's faith; — think of Joan d'Arc!
Oh, ne'er was cause more holy, or ne'er could man or maid
More freely lift the *heart* to God with *hand* upon the blade.

For we fight against injustice, and, in every battle won,
We have struck a blow for freedom, and a world is looking on;
Yet still waters run the deepest, and 'tis not alone by war
That the greatest good's accomplished — silent influence's better far.

Let no selfish love restrain you, — *country first*, and then our friends;
What is one without the other? Would you clasp a coward's hand?
While our brothers toil in battle, we who stay at home can pray;
And our God, the God of battles, he will give the victory.

Few things are more noticeable now than the prevalence of mourning. You cannot stand in any crowded assembly without remarking this. One day on the street you meet smiling faces, — they have come from the post-office perhaps, and *that letter* has made their sunshine, — then over the swift wires comes the news of victory, and lo! there passes you a figure in black, coarse black, most likely, — for the pay of a common soldier will not buy fine crape for the mourners. There is no display of sorrow, no pageantry of grief to tell the world, at large, they have lost a friend, — only a quiet changing from the gay garb of yesterday to the shadowy one of to-day.

Oh, these sad-eyed, pale-faced figures, in black, pass by us more frequently than they did years ago, and in their sorrow lies a deeper meaning! What *they* have lost has been sacrificed for the benefit of a nation; and a nation shares their grief.

" Oh, when the fight is won,
Dear land whom triflers now make bold to scorn,
Thee, from whose forehead earth awaits her morn,
How nobler does the sun
Flame in thy sky! how braver breathes thy air,
That thou hadst children who for thee couldst dare
And die as thine have done!

IN MEMORIAM.

Sunlight upon a new-made grave,
And turf above the breast
Of one who stood among us once,
As student and as guest.

"More light! more light!" this dying wish
  Of Goethe's poet soul
Found echo on thy lips, O friend!
  Found echo in *thy* soul.

God heard; he always hears the prayers
  Of those, whose lives are given
To country and to him; he sent
  The eternal light of heaven.

Yes, it is well, — let the same old bell,
  That in the days gone by
Rang out to him the hours of time,
  Ring in, — eternity.

Who next shall fall for country's honor?
Who next shall sleep 'neath the starry banner?
God pity the mothers, and pity all
For whom the sheen of sunshine shall fall
On a vacant chair, a desolate home,
And the new-made grave of a friend!

BREVITY.

Brevity is the soul of wit. It is also the true test of wisdom. Cæsar's "veni, vidi, vici," has lived, and will live, because it is short, sharp, and full of meaning. It was Milton — was it not? — who being requested to put Christ's miracle at the marriage-feast into poetry, expressed it all in one immortal line?

"The conscious water saw its God, and blushed."

People who stayed at home, and made long and loud professions of loyalty, were not apt to be the truest patriots. You remember that sublime verse in Genesis, which describes the creation: "And God said, let there be light, and there was light." Do you also recollect how rhetoric speaks of one who thus gives the same idea in many words: "The Sovereign Arbiter of the universe, by the potent energy of a single word, commanded light to exist, and immediately it sprang into being?" Mark the change. Such "linked sweetness, long drawn out," is anything but pleasing.

Of what avail a long lecture, or sermon, or even prayer, except to weary or disgust the hearer?

Religion does not consist in many and high-sounding words; but is best shown in those little, decisive *acts* of every-day life. No man ever made his words immortal who did not make them brief.

Scripture commands are always short and comprehensive. The Lord's Prayer is short; and no superfluous words can be found in the ten commandments.

The shortest verse in the Bible is one of the most affecting. "Jesus wept!" What could be more touching? The King of Glory mourning over fallen man!

A FRAGMENT.

Past, Present, and Future, — Oh, what is there here
That is worth one regret, one lingering tear?
When the summons is given, — O spirit, return
To the hands of thy Giver — poor wanderer come home, —
We mourn not, we weep not, for that which is fled;
Though our tears fall like rain on the face of the dead,
They are tears for the living, for those who alone
Over life's weary pathway must still wander on.
Yet courage faint heart! to thee comfort is given,
For the dear ones who've left us are happy in heaven.
We shall miss their sweet presence, and yearn for their love,
Yet, sometime, God helping, we'll meet them above.

MYSTERY.

There once was a dove, — in her nest,
Seven birdlings chirped; and three
Were weak as weak could be;
Three strong, — and one the best
And dearest of the seven,
He plumed his wings for heaven.
And the mother-bird wept. O mystery!
It is all as sad as sad can be.
    'Tis a mystery all.

There once was a ship, — she sailed
Where the tide-waves ebb and flow,
And laughed at the storm; when, lo!
Snapped every sail, rent by the gale,
Bent every mast 'neath slavery's blast;
Her future seemed to mock her past.
God knows the fate of our bonnie boat,
The Union, — will it ever float
    As before? To us 'tis a mystery.

When creeds are confused, and in strife
Stand the guides to the Heavenly Feast,
And he who reads most knows the least
Of the way, — who shall wonder if Life,
Young Life, all aglow for the fight,
Be wearied with waiting for light?
Who shall blame if it falters, and who if it falls?
Let God judge. To us 'tis a mystery all,
    And we cannot know.

There were once two friends, — two friends
Who loved each other so,
That when God bade one go,

The other prayed, — Oh, send
Some token if the soul
That has reached the heavenly goal
Holds dear to his heart the left behind !
O mystery ! ye fools and blind,
   Ye cannot know.

There was once a slender vine,
Planted on the brow of this Hill,
And it flourisheth there still,
Grown strong. Its tendrils twine
Round right; its fruit through all these years
Has fallen midst a fall of tears;
We can but wonder as it grows.
We ask its future. Well, God knows.
   To us 'tis a mystery.

There's a stream, 'tis deep and wide;
Who near it, oft repine;
Who cross it, make no sign
When they reach the other side.
Dark is the hither shore.
Though each one must pass o'er,
And fain would know why they must go,
And where, and whence its waters flow;
   'Tis a mystery all.

There were once eight sticks, all found
In the Pine-Tree State; some straight,
Some were crooked, and strange to relate,
Since they grew on such similar ground;
Some were bending as willows when breezes blow;
Some unyielding as granite. Now, tell me, who knows,
Why they grafted themselves on the tree of knowledge,
And came *en masse* to the Wesleyan College ?
   For to us 'tis a mystery.

The following was prepared for her graduation piece in 1866 : —

THE STUDENT'S REWARD.

Since the world began, rewards and punishments have been distributed with an impartial hand by their great Author. The mother smiles approvingly upon the first warm impulse that prompts her little one's heart to deeds of kindness. The world bows in homage before its own great men ; and God himself on those he loves showers blessings. We all look forward to the reward which is to be ours, and choose our life-work according to that which promises most.

With the various dispositions of mankind, there must ever be an infinite diversity of tastes ; but, —

such productions as are here given of her early and later writings; although a large number were lost with other things at the Hill. We regret the loss of one of her ablest productions, written soon after she went to the Hill,— title, *Ancient and Modern Chivalry;* and if any person who shall read this, has, or knows of any one who has, a copy of that article, we should be greatly obliged for a copy of the same.

In closing, permit me to say to all who shall have patience to read this narrative through, that with much research and toil, I have gathered up the evidence and circumstances from which I have based my conclusions, and, in pamphlet form, lay them before the public; asking the public journalists of the State, if the fact comes to their knowledge that I have made a statement of this sad case, to notice the same in their journals. *Justice* will give such notice a place in those papers which published the reports of committees on the other side from Kent's Hill. In view of all that has transpired on the Hill, and the course Torsey has pursued towards Louise while under his care and since she died, his disposition shown to, and the treatment of her friends, I must say, I loath and detest this miserable compound of intrigue and deception, and desire him to be kept out of my sight and mind if possible. I will not attempt to call him deserved names, as I can find no terms in the English language that will do him justice.

I cannot pass unnoticed that whole-souled class-mate of Louise, Adelaide Webb, who, untrammelled by religious creeds, speaks out fully her true sentiments without fear, and says, "I have long wished for some avenue through which to express my esteem and love for Louise," etc. (See her letter in full on page 61.)

"THE CROWN WON, BUT NOT WORN,"

Was the title of Louise's exhibition piece, prepared and read by her on the stage, in June, 1865, in regard to the life and death of the lamented Lincoln. Its length precludes its publication here.

Being forcibly impressed with that title, and her effort, and their sudden exit from earthly scenes, caused me to adopt that title.

The following lines of a distinguished poet are applicable to the close of this sad narrative,—

> "Man's inhumanity to man
> Makes countless millions mourn."

www.ingramcontent.com/pod-product-compliance
Lightning Source LLC
Chambersburg PA
CBHW030305170426
43202CB00009B/881